Pam Wedgwood

© 2006 by Faber Music Ltd
First published in 2006 by Faber Music Ltd
3 Queen Square London WC1N 3AU
Cover design by Stik
Music processed by MusicSet 2000
Printed in England by Caligraving Ltd
All rights reserved

ISBN 0-571-52420-6

To buy Faber Music publications or to find out about the full range of titles available
please contact your local music retailer or Faber Music sales enquiries:

Faber Music Limited, Burnt Mill, Elizabeth Way, Harlow CM20 2HX
Tel: +44 (0)1279 82 89 82   Fax: +44 (0)1279 82 89 83
sales@fabermusic.com   fabermusic.com

1. Imaginary friends

2. Downtown groove

With a groovy beat! ♩ = 126

3. Fly-trap

4. Pipkin

With a relaxed feel ♩ = 102

5. The Bumbles

In bumble-march time! ♩ = 116 – 120

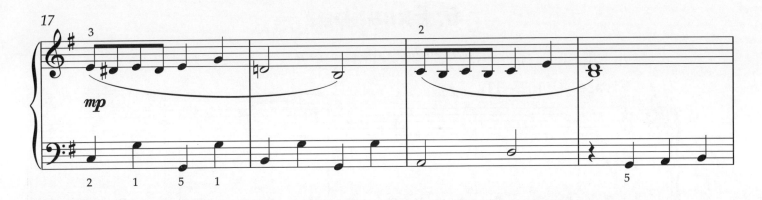

poco rit.   a tempo

Musical-box style

6. Excalibur

King Arthur's magic sword

marcato

7. Bonzo doo-dah

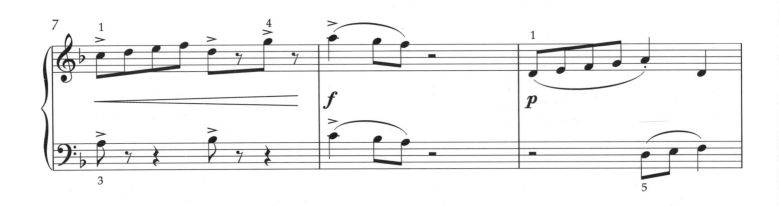

8. Daylight disco

14

9. Down in the jungle

10. Honky-tonk man

Lively, with a solid beat ♩ = 120

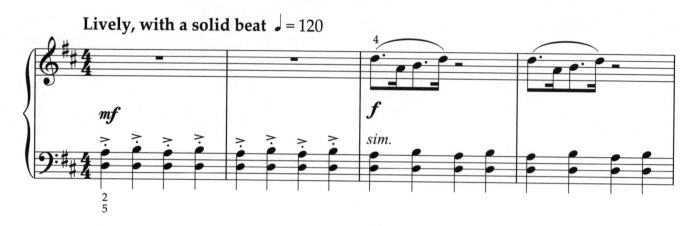

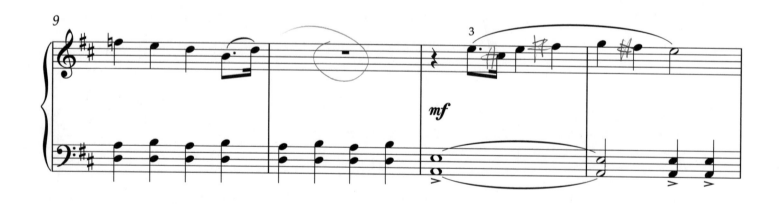

11. Soulful reggae

12. Gregory Griggs

Gregory Griggs, Gregory Griggs, Had twenty seven different wigs.
He wore them up, he wore them down, To please the people of the town;
He wore them east, he wore them west, But he could never tell which he liked best!

Jauntily ♩ = 144 – 152 (*or as fast as you can!*)

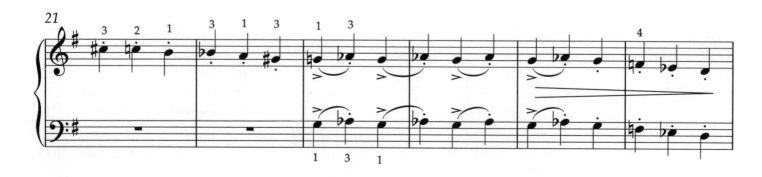

13. Soldier, soldier

14. Mystic Meg

The Game is Up

Book 3

We believe that the Bible is God's word to mankind, and that it contains everything we need to know in order to be reconciled with God and live in a way that is pleasing to him. Therefore, we believe it is vital to teach children accurately from the Bible, being careful to teach each passage's true meaning in an appropriate way for children, rather than selecting a 'children's message' from a Biblical passage.

Copyright 2003 © TnT Ministries
29 Buxton Gardens, Acton, London, W3 9LE
Tel: +44 (0) 20 8992 0450 Fax: +44 (0) 20 8896 1847

Contributors: Trevor Blundell; Thalia Blundell; John Chamberlain; Carolyn Chamberlain; Annie Gemmill; Guy Lachlan; Kirsteen McCulloch; Kathy Pierce

Published in 2003 by Christian Focus Publications Ltd.
Geanies House, Fearn, Tain, Ross-shire, IV20 1TW
Tel: 01862 871 011 Fax: 01862 871 699
email: info@christianfocus.com

Cover design by Tim Charnick
Illustrations by Tim Charnick
Printed by Arrowsmith

ISBN 1-85792-820-2

Contents

Introduction

The great desire of our hearts is that children everywhere will come to love and trust Jesus as their Lord and Saviour. It is our firm belief that this happens primarily through the teaching of God's word in the Bible. This book of games and ideas is designed as a resource to complement and support Bible teaching. It has been written as a companion volume to the 'On the Way' Bible teaching programme, but is suitable for use in any situation where the Bible is being taught to children.

Teaching the Bible is an exacting task. Teaching the Bible to children is even more so. The concepts are sometimes hard to communicate and are often contrary to the norms in the secular society in which they live. They are used to an interactive style of learning and they want to have fun. Traditionally we have tended to separate off the 'Bible teaching' slot from the rest of the activities in our children's programmes which are fun but have no Bible content. How much better to make every part of the programme count in the teaching of God's word! Since children learn by repetition, why teach something once when you can teach it several times, using all the activities and games to contribute to the learning process? In this way not only is learning enhanced but the Bible is exciting, relevant and truly central to the group's activities.

In this book we have outlined 3 supplementary activities - the Warm Up, the Consolidation and the Wind Up. Though this is only one model of an integrated teaching approach, it has been used by TnT Ministries with great success for many years. We have found consistently that with this kind of repetition even the smallest child can learn big things about God.

Warm Up

This is a short activity or presentation designed to arrest the attention of the children and prepare them for the Bible teaching which is to follow.

Consolidation

This is a constructive game or activity designed to reinforce the key concepts, theme, aim or details of the Bible story that has just been taught. It generally involves plenty of physical activity and some simple equipment.

Wind Up

A Wind Up is the final summation of the days teaching. It involves linking the Warm Up, the Bible story and the Consolidation together, emphasising the central teaching point.

Warm ups and wind ups take around 5 minutes and a Consolidation game 10-15 minutes. For each Bible story there are 2 schemes of Warm Ups, Consolidations and Wind Ups described. One will often require more space or more equipment. The ideas and suggestions in this book are only guidelines for you to adapt and change in line with the age, number and needs of your children and limitations of your meeting space. We would stress that they should be used alongside, not in place of, teaching directly from the Bible. In some warm ups the leader demonstrates negative qualities, such as favouritism. When acting out of character we suggest that you don a hat or jacket, or call yourself a different name, so that the younger children do not equate the bad points with the leader.

The Purpose of Miracles

Many New Testament stories deal with miracles. It is important that the children are taught clearly the difference between miracles and magic. Miracles show God restoring or creating in line with his nature and are signs that God is at work. They take place when God acts in the natural order in an unusual manner and their occurrence are predicted and/or take place at the command or prayer of God's messenger.

The purpose of miracles is:
- to bring glory to God (John 2:11; 11:4)
- to authenticate the ministry of the person performing them (John 3:2)
- to lead the observer(s) to faith in God (John 20:30-31, Acts 9:36-42)
- to deepen the faith of the believers.

True miracles always harmonise with the rest of Scripture in their portrayal of God's character. Magic, on the other hand, is always to do with illusion and deception. i.e. to trick or fool the observer(s).

Creating your own Games

Why not create your own games, custom made to serve your children, and take advantage of the special possibilities of your meeting place? It's easy if you take account of a few basic principles. The first task is to spend time in the Bible. Your game is a teaching opportunity and you need to understand the message of your passage for the day before you will know the concept, aim or details you want to teach from it via the game. There are four important elements to designing and running successful games.

Rules

There need to be SIMPLE RULES which are easily understood and which can be enforced to make the game fun, safe, workable and educational.

- Explain the rules, then ask questions to see if they have understood them. Then ask if they have any questions before repeating the rules and starting the game. This may sound laborious but it is a good investment of time.

- Start the game with a clear command, e.g. 'When I say GO', or, 'When I drop my hand'.

- The rules must be applied consistently and rule breakers need to be dealt with firmly.

Participation

Games are for joining in, not for watching, and so good games involve lots of participation. To make a game fun for everyone, as many children as possible need to be on the move at the same time. However, a safe environment must be preserved at all times.

- Games involving cross movements of children or games depending on speed alone are best avoided.

- Small or otherwise vulnerable children must be protected. Sometimes it is possible to design a game where these children have a different role from the older ones. All children should be encouraged to take part but never forced.

- It is wise to have a strategy for stopping the game and restoring order if necessary. The command 'Statues' or 'Freeze' will do this. A 'Sin Bin' is also useful for rule breakers.

A Scoring System

A scoring system is needed to determine who wins. Children are naturally competitive and learning to win and lose graciously is a valuable social skill. However:

- It must be absolutely fair and administered by an impartial adult.

- It must be understandable, preferably visual.

- All efforts should be affirmed and congratulated. A running commentary by the game leader is very helpful.

Equipment

Equipment of some sort is needed for nearly all games. Children like to hold, carry and hide things.

- Almost anything can be used in games, but it must be safe. It is unwise to include anything which might be used as a weapon.

- It should be easy to reset if necessary during the game and easy to clear up at the end.

- The ideal is to have a small store of safe, versatile items for use in your games.

List of suggested items

Balloons & blow-up items	Empty plastic soft drink bottles	Soft sponge balls
Balls of string	Newspapers	Sponges
Buckets	Small items to act as tokens	Table tennis balls
Cardboard boxes	e.g. bottle tops, corks, buttons	
Cardboard tubes	Plastic jar lids	
Clothes-lines x 18m. lengths	Plastic laundry baskets or sledges	
Dried peas, beans, lentils, etc.	Puppets - two - one boy - one girl	
Disposable or plastic cups	Sheet or parachute	

REASSURED BY AN ANGEL

Text: Read and study Matthew 1:18-25

Teaching Point: God confirms that Jesus is the promised Saviour.

WARM-UP 1

Prior to the lesson write the children's names in a column on a flipchart or board. Prepare a list of occupations, one per child, writing each one on a strip of card. Place the occupation cards with a wooden cross in a box and gift wrap it. Occupations can include doctor, nurse, astronaut, teacher, rubbish collector, belly dancer, ice cream taster, secret agent, etc.

Today's true story from the Bible is about a baby whose job had been chosen for him before he was born. Come back and tell me:

1 Who was the baby?

2 What was the job?

3 How did the baby's parents know what job he would do?

CONSOLIDATION 1

Divide the children into teams and provide each team with an identical newspaper. The leader calls out something that can be found in the newspaper, such as a crossword, something about a toy, something about a celebrity, etc. The first team to find the item waves the page in the air. Points are given for each item found.

WIND-UP 1

Remind the children that they do not know what job they will grow up to do. Go over the questions from the warm-up. Link into the game. Did God send the news to Joseph in a newspaper? How did the leader know that the children had listened to him in the game? How do we know that Joseph listened to the angel? (He took Mary as his wife.) End by pointing out how Jesus did the job he came to do - he died on the cross. This is the best Christmas present we could have.

Show the present to the children and open it. Bring out the cross. What a strange present. Look in the box and find the strips of card. Point out that they contain different jobs. Ask the child at the bottom of the list to draw a job out of the box for the child at the top of the list. Stick the card on the board against the child at the top of the list. Continue with each child picking an occupation card for the next child on the list. Did they all get the job they want to do?

REASSURED BY AN ANGEL

Text: Read and study Matthew 1:18-25

Teaching Point: God confirms that Jesus is the promised Saviour.

WARM-UP 2

Leader 1 sets out a line of plastic cups on a table and places a small object under one of them. He shuffles the cups around and asks the children to identify the cup containing the object. Repeat the exercise.

Whilst this is going on Leader 2 comes in with a small envelope on which is written, 'I have a message for you.' Leader 2 gives the envelope to Leader 1, who reads out the writing on the envelope then places it in his pocket saying, 'I'll look at it later.' Leader 2 exits and Leader 1 continues with the cups activity.

Leader 2 enters with a bigger envelope on which is written, 'Open immediately!' He gives it to Leader 1, who ignores it as before. 'I'm busy. It'll have to wait.' Leader 2 exits and Leader 1 continues with the cups activity.

Either Leader 2 or Leader 3 enters wearing a motorcycle helmet and carrying an enormous envelope plus a clip board and pen. Leader 1 has to sign for the envelope and open it there and then. Leader 1 opens the envelope, 'reads' the letter, cries out, 'Oh no!' and runs out.

Leader 2/3 says, 'In today's true story from the Bible we will find out how God sent a very important message to someone.' Send them to Bible time with the following questions:

1. Who received the message?

2. How do we know the message was important? *It was sent by an angel.*

3. What was the message?

CONSOLIDATION 2

The aim of the consolidation is to reinforce the message that Jesus is the promised Saviour. Divide the children into equal teams and have a relay race. Each team is divided in half with one half stationed at the beginning point and the other half at the end. It is helpful if a leader is stationed with each group of children. The leader at the beginning whispers the message, 'Jesus is the promised Saviour' to child A. Child A runs to the other end and whispers the same message to child B. Child B runs back to the beginning and whispers the message to child C. The game continues until all the children have had a turn. The last child whispers the message to the leader at that end. The winner is the first team to complete the course and whisper the correct message to the leader. If the average age of the children is under 7 you might want to simplify the message by removing 'promised'.

WIND-UP 2

Remind the children of the warm-up and go over the questions. Talk about the game and the message sent.

THE WISE MEN'S GIFTS TO JESUS

Text: Read and study Matthew 2:1-12

Teaching Point: Jesus is king and is to be worshipped.

WARM-UP 1

Place 3 gifts in gift wrapped boxes on a table. Ask the children to tell you about the presents they received for Christmas. Point out the 3 presents on the table. They are presents you received. What could be in them? Open up the presents one at a time to reveal the contents. Ask the children to say whether or not they like the present by thumbs up / thumbs down or cheering / booing. Point out that some gifts are more acceptable than others. (It is helpful if one of the gifts represents something in the Bible story, such as a star and one is something that the children would not want, such as a piece of mouldy cheese.)

In today's true story from the Bible we will find out about some gifts, some of which were very strange. Come back and tell me:

1. What were the gifts?
2. What did the gifts represent?
3. Which of my gifts can be found in the story?

CONSOLIDATION 1

Designate 3 locations, 1 marked by a crown, 1 by a cross and 1 by 'God'. At each location place a series of Christmas cards face down. Some of the Christmas cards should contain accurate pictures of the Christmas story and some should contain other things, such as snow scenes, robins, etc. The children start in the centre. Go over the answers to the warm-up questions and make sure that the children understand the significance of the 3 gifts. When the leader calls out, 'Gold!' the children all run to the crown location. When 'Frankincense!' is called the children run to the 'God' location and when 'Myrrh!' is called they run to the cross.

The game can be played as an elimination one with the last x number of children arriving at the

location declared out. It can also be varied by calling out a location, then calling another one just as the main body of the group reaches the first location called. Sometimes the location can be whispered, rather than called out. At some point in the game ask the children to turn over the cards at each location and sort out which ones are about the Christmas story and which are not.

WIND-UP 1

Emphasise what the wise men came to do - find the king of the Jews, worship him and give him presents. Recap on the significance of the 3 gifts. Were they the sort of gifts you would normally give to a baby? Point back to the warm-up and the appropriateness or otherwise of those gifts. Which gift in the warm-up was also in the Bible story?

THE WISE MEN'S GIFTS TO JESUS

Text: Read and study Matthew 2:1-12

Teaching Point: Jesus is king and is to be worshipped.

WARM-UP 2

Leader tells the children about his grandmother. My gran is having her 80th birthday. She lives in (specify a country a long way away), so I don't see her very often. I haven't seen her for 5 years. Her family are giving her a special party and I really want to be there. How am I going to get there? Ask the children to help work out the journey. Taxi to the station, train to the airport, plane, coach from the airport to the local town where you will be collected by the family in their car. Show the children all the different tickets you will need. (Collect old tickets or make them.) Discover that some of the tickets are missing. The children help find the missing tickets. Ask the children if that is all you need. No, you have a present for granny. Show the children a wrapped present.

Today's true story from the Bible is about some people who made a very long journey to see someone special. Come back and tell me:

1. Who made the journey?
2. Who was the special person?
3. What presents did they take?

CONSOLIDATION 2

Line all the children up with the leader at the head. They are going on a long journey, stopping at different staging points. (These can be indicated by mats.) Leader calls out the method of transport between each staging post and demonstrates suitable actions for the children to copy, e.g. stick arms out at the sides for an aeroplane, rowing action for a boat, etc. Each method of transport has a different associated action. At each staging post stop, make a circle and ask the children a question about the story. Then line up and continue to the next staging post.

WIND-UP 2

Remind the children of the warm-up and recap on the questions asked. Go over what the gifts symbolised and what they tell us about Jesus.

GUIDED BY A STAR

Text: Matthew 2:1-12

Teaching Point: Jesus is king and is to be worshipped.

WARM-UP 1

Display a selection of items and ask the children to separate those that are to do with guides from those that are not. Suggested items (guide) dog, road map, park ranger, museum guide, car, orange, lighthouse, etc.

Today's true story from the Bible tells us how God guided some people. Come back and tell me:

1. Who did God guide?

2. How many methods of guidance were used? *Two - a star and an angel.*

CONSOLIDATION 1

Treasure hunt. Divide the children into small groups consisting of 1 leader (or older child) and 3-4 children. Devise a series of clues to take the children from place to place in the class area. You might want the children to answer a question from the story at each place before they move on to the next place. The clues/questions are written on stars which are placed in 8 different locations. The stars should be coded in some way so that each group can distinguish their own stars. Each location contains the same number of stars as there are groups of children.

Give each group their first clue/question. The leader asks his group the question. When he gets the answer he follows the instruction attached to that question, e.g. go to the big table and collect your star. The process is repeated as each new star is collected. It is preferable if each group collects from locations in a different order: e.g.

```
team A: 1  3  5  7  2  4  6  8
team B: 2  4  6  8  3  5  7  1
team C: 3  5  7  1  4  6  8  2
team D: 4  6  8  2  5  7  1  3
```

Each group's final star should point to the same place where a nativity scene has been set up.

WIND-UP 1

Wind up at the nativity scene. Go over the warm-up and the answers to the questions. Discuss why God guided the wise men to Jesus. Point out that Jesus came to save everyone - Gentiles as well as Jews. Recap on the significance of the gifts.

GUIDED BY A STAR

Text: Matthew 2:1-12

Teaching Point: Jesus is king and is to be worshipped.

WARM-UP 2

Show the children a selection of items that require a response, such as a sandwich/cake (needs eating), a cuddly toy (needs cuddling), a football (needs kicking), a monster (needs running away from), etc. As you show the children each item ask, 'What's the best/right thing to do with this?'

Today's true story from the Bible is about the right way to treat someone who is very special. Come back and tell me:

1. Who is the special person?
2. How should that person be treated and why?

CONSOLIDATION 2

A journey game. Divide the children into 2 teams. Mark out a winding course with 2 lines of rope or masking tape approximately 1 metre apart. Halfway along the course place a chair with a box containing a few sponge balls or balls of newspaper. The teams line up at the same end of the course. Each member of team A is given a sponge ball (or ball of newspaper). On the command, 'Go!' the first child in each team runs the length of the course. When the team A child reaches the box he drops his ball into it then continues to the end of the course. When the child from Team B reaches the box he picks up a ball before continuing to the end of the course. The second child in each team races once the first child has reached the box. Once all the children in the team have reached their destination the race is reversed with the children in team A picking up their balls from the box and the children from team B depositing their balls in the box. The first team to get all its members back to the start wins.

If you have a group of older children the race can be made more difficult by making any child who steps outside the lines return to the start of that leg of the race.

WIND-UP 2

Use the game to link into the Wise Men's journey. They did not have lines to guide them on the right way. Remind the children of the warm-up and go over the questions. Talk about how we worship Jesus.

Lesson 3

WARNED BY AN ANGEL

Text: Matthew 2:13-23

Teaching Point: God's plan cannot be thwarted.

Memory verse: *Jesus is the Saviour of the world. John 4:42*

WARM-UP 1

This is designed to focus the children's attention on warnings. Display pictures of different methods of warning, e.g. road sign for school (children crossing), road sign for falling rocks, sign saying, 'Danger! thin ice', police car with flashing light, fire engine with siren, lifeboat on stormy sea, lighthouse, etc. Talk about warnings - why we need them, different kinds, etc., using the pictures as visual aids, (see page 50).

In today's true story from the Bible we will find out about a warning. Come back and tell me:

1. Who gave the warning?

2. How was the warning given?

3. What was the warning about?

CONSOLIDATION 1

Prior to the lesson prepare sets of 7 cards with one word on each card, such as 'Jesus is the Saviour of the world', 'Jesus is the reason for the season', 'A Christmas without Jesus is a turkey', 'Jesus is the very best Christmas present'. Mark the first and last cards of each phrase by using a capital letter for the first word and a full stop after the last one. Divide the children into teams of 7 plus a leader. Each team requires one set of cards. (For large groups some sets may need to be duplicated.) Give each team a set of 7 questions on the Bible story. As each question is answered correctly a child runs to the end of the room and collects one card. The first team to collect all their cards and put them into the correct order wins.

WIND-UP 1

Look at the different sets of cards collected in the game. Discuss their meaning and teach the memory verse. Recap on the warm-up and go over the answer to the questions. Point out that God was in control and he made sure that Jesus escaped from Herod.

WARM-UP 2

Leader 1 decides to make a cake. He puts on an apron and gets out a selection of utensils and ingredients, such as a measuring spoon, a mixing spoon, a spatula, 2 different size bowls, a measuring jug, a cup, scales, some butter, flour, eggs, mixed fruit, etc. Leader 1 starts to make his cake. Leader 2 enters and takes a utensil. Leader 1 carries on by using something else. The process is repeated until Leader 1 is unable to continue and says, 'I cannot carry on making my cake because all my equipment has been taken. I've been prevented from doing it. All my plans have come to nothing.'

In today's true story from the Bible we will see what happens when someone tries to prevent God's plan from coming to pass. Come back and tell me:

1. What was God's plan? *To save the world through Jesus.*

2. Who tried to prevent it and how? *Herod, by ordering the killing of the boys under 2.*

3. How did God stop his plan from being prevented?

CONSOLIDATION 2

A thwarting game. Divide the children into teams. Give them the appropriate equipment to complete a series of tasks. Tell the children that they are competing against each other each time. Once they have commenced a task, leaders disrupt it each time.

Suggested tasks: building a tower, making a path from A to B, setting up a tent.

WIND-UP 2

Discuss the difficulties the teams experienced during the game. Refer to the warm-up and go over the answers to the questions.

PREPARING THE MESSENGER

Text: Matthew 4:1-11, Mark 1:9-13

Teaching Point: Jesus identified with those he came to save.

WARM-UP 1

Place a washing up bowl containing water on the table. Talk about washing dirty things to make them clean. Demonstrate with a variety of dirty items. Finish with a doll with a dirty face. Point out that we have baths to make us clean. Does it make us clean inside?

Today's true story from the Bible is about someone who went into the water and it wasn't to have a bath or to swim. Come back and tell me:

1. Who went into the water?
2. Why?

CONSOLIDATION 1

Divide the children into small groups of not more than 5. Give each group a bowl of water on a large piece of plastic sheet, sponges, tooth brushes, tea towels and a selection of dirty items. Suggested items are vegetables such as potatoes, dirty toys, stones, shells, etc. The groups can have a different combination of items. Once the items have been cleaned the children clean up their area and make a display of the cleaned items. Each group is judged to see how well they have done.

WIND-UP 1

Talk about cleaning dirty items, referring to the game and warm-up. Go over the questions in the warm-up. Point out that baptism is a sign of being made clean; the water cannot make a person clean on the inside, only Jesus can do that. Tell the children that Christians are still baptised as a sign of belonging to God's family. Talk about the different ways of doing it.

WARM-UP 2

Unwind a length of rope and join the 2 ends to make a circle. Sit all the children in a circle holding onto the rope. Ask them to lift the rope up. Point out that the rope is one thing that is joining them together. Put the rope down and discuss what other things we all have in common, such as being people, living in the same area (specify),

going to the same church, etc. Finish with all being tempted to do naughty things - even the leaders, their parents and the church minister. Give examples of being tempted, e.g.

- when we have broken something we are tempted to lie to get out of trouble,
- when we see a piece of chocolate that belongs to someone else we are tempted to steal it,
- when we've been tagged in the game we are tempted to cheat by pretending we have not been tagged.

We've talked about 3 different sorts of temptations. Today's true story from the Bible is about someone who had 3 different temptations. Come back and tell me:

1. Who was it?
2. What was he tempted to do?

CONSOLIDATION 2

Place a tray in the centre of the room containing a mix of wrapped sweets and bottle tops or other tokens. You need at least double the amount of tokens as children present. Spread mats or sheets of newspaper around the room. The children move around to music only stepping on the mats or newspaper. If a child steps off the mat or newspaper he goes into the sin bin for 1 turn. When the music stops the children run into the centre, pick up a token from the tray and return to the same mat. Then they make their way, only stepping on the mats, to any leader and balance their token on any part of the leader. If the token falls off that child goes to the sin bin for 1 turn. The children return to any mat and the game restarts. Any child taking a sweet rather than a token goes to the sin bin for 2 turns.

WIND-UP 2

Talk about giving in to temptation, linking in to the temptation to pick up a sweet during the game. Go over the questions from the warm-up. Talk about how Jesus helps us not to give in to temptation.

THE LORD'S PRAYER

Text: Matthew 6:5-15

Teaching Point: God always answers his people's prayers.

WARM-UP 1

To demonstrate that communication equipment is no good unless someone answers the caller. You need a selection of items of communication equipment, such as a telephone, a loudspeaker/loudhailer, megaphone, a microphone, a drum, a whistle, Morse code key (or tap out a code), flags for semaphore, newspaper, advertising poster, torch or flashlight, letter or correspondence, message in a bottle, telegram, a picture of Indian smoke signals, fax machine. Use the actual items suggested or picture representations of the communication types.

Display the items in clear view of the children. If you have a telephone with a BT cord, attach the telecom plug to a piece of blue-tak under the table so that it appears operative. Ask the children if they know what all the items on the table have in common. They are all used for communication.

Take each item, one by one, and explain how it works. Select the telephone last, dial a number and wait for a reply. No one answers. Dial again. Same result - no reply. Ask the children if they have phoned someone and received no answer?

In today's true story from the Bible we will learn about someone who is always there to hear his people when they call to him.

CONSOLIDATION 1

To demonstrate that sometimes we have to wait for guidance. It requires careful listening, patience and strict following of instructions.

Equipment: a whistle, one or two blindfolds suitable for a child, a ribbon to designate the chosen sheep.

Choose a leader to be the shepherd and a child to be the sheepdog. All the remaining children are sheep. The shepherd nominates a sheep to be caught and attaches a ribbon to it. Talk about how sheep move round and move away from the sheepdog. The shepherd instructs the children to move around on all fours like sheep while the sheepdog watches where they are going. After a short interval the shepherd tells

the sheep to stand still. Then he blind folds the sheepdog. The sheepdog has to find the nominated sheep. The shepherd will call out instructions to the sheepdog only when it asks, 'Which way?' Occasionally the shepherd blows the whistle, which is a signal for the sheep to move around to a new position before standing still again. The sheepdog starts the process again by asking, 'Which way?' Change the sheepdog after a set time limit or if it finds the nominated sheep. If you have a large group of children you may want to have 2 shepherds and 2 sheepdogs going after the same sheep at the same time.

Lesson 6

THE LORD'S PRAYER

Text: Matthew 6:5-15

Teaching Point: God always answers his people's prayers.

WIND-UP 1

Refer to the warm-up and how communication equipment is no good unless someone answers. Does God always answer when his people pray? Refer to the game and how the sheep dog had to wait for answers from the shepherd. We ask for direction (answers) in prayer and sometimes the answers are not what we expect or are not immediate, but God always answers our prayers in the way that is best for us.

WARM-UP 2

To show how easy it is to fall into temptation and who we can call to for help.

Use a skit or puppet (see script on page 71). Attach an empty Smarties packet (or similar) to the puppet's hand.

Toby appears with the packet of Smarties. The leader asks him what he's got and where he got it from. Toby says he has borrowed the sweets, but when asked how many he has to give back shakes the packet to find it is empty. It then transpires that Toby found the sweets on a table at the leader's house. When asked if he was given permission to take the sweets Toby states that he asked Jughead, who said yes. Jughead is a little voice that Toby hears in his head and tells him it is right to do naughty things. The leader then asks Toby why he listens to a voice telling him to do the wrong things. Toby replies that he does not know who else to listen to.

In today's true story from the Bible we will learn whom we should talk to whenever we have a problem.

CONSOLIDATION 2

Place 4 chairs, one on each side of the room and equidistant from each other. Put a double sheet or parachute in the centre of the room. The children are rabbits leaving the warren, (symbolised by the sheet), and going to the feeding areas (symbolised by the 4 chairs). These are the only safe areas. One of the leaders is designated as the fox. The fox has 2 or 3 inflated balloons with which to tag the children when they are told to leave or return to the warren. Both the main leader and the fox call instructions to the rabbits. The rabbits only have to obey the main leader. Any rabbit who is tagged is out. You could add more foxes if this will add more excitement to the game.

WIND-UP 2

Remind the children of the warm-up and the importance of listening to the right person when tempted to do the wrong thing. Who is the Tempter? Who will help us to escape? Refer to the game and how easy it was to get caught out. God is not like the main leader. When he tells us to do things he never gets it wrong.

THE TWO HOUSES

Text: Matthew 7:24-29

Teaching Point: Listen and obey.

WARM-UP 1

Leader 1 instructs the children to do what he does. Perform various exercises, such as star jumps, press-ups, running on the spot. Finish with the children in a line following Leader 1 around the room. The remaining leaders have been primed not to join in. Leader 1 draws attention to this, asking the other leaders to take part. They still do not join in. At the end Leader 1 gives all the children a reward, but the leaders miss out.

Today's true story from the Bible is about the importance of doing what Jesus said.

CONSOLIDATION 1

The leaders hold up a parachute or double sheet in the centre of the room. Each child is given one of six designators linked to the story, such as sand, cement, brick, mortar, stone, roof. The children stand around the outside of the parachute. The leaders flap the parachute up and down. When Leader 1 calls out a designator, those children run under the parachute to the other side. More than one designator can be called at a time. Whenever Leader 1 calls, 'Walls!' all the children run to the nearest wall and remain there until told to return to stand near the parachute. Any child who does not run when their designator is called misses a turn.

WIND-UP 1

Remind the children of the warm-up and how only those who did what the leader said were included in the reward. Refer to the game and what happened to those who did not obey the leader's commands. Recap on the details of the parable and the importance of obeying Jesus.

WARM-UP 2

Tell the children to watch what you are doing. Build 2 bases, one of 4 Bibles and one of sponges, bread rolls or something similar.

Show the children a tray containing some heavy items. Which base will support the weight?

Today's true story from the Bible is about the importance of building on the right base.

CONSOLIDATION 2

Divide the children into groups, each group with a leader. Give each group different equipment for building a house, such as cardboard boxes, mats, sheets, wooden bricks. Allocate each group to an area. Some build their houses on the floor and some on a sheet or blanket. The houses do not need to be big enough for the children to get inside. After they have finished the children show their houses to each other. Finally, everyone pulls on the blanket or sheet and watches those houses fall down.

WIND-UP 2

Refer to the game. Point out that it was not how the houses were built that was important but what they were built on. This was the same in the warm-up. Recap on the details of the parable. What did Jesus say was the right base for us to build our lives on?

THE SOWER

Text: Matthew 13:1-23

Teaching Point: The need to respond to God's word and to put it into practice.

WARM-UP 1

Prepare 6 cards, each one containing a different number from 1 to 6. Also prepare some cards that give options, such as 2G & 1B (2 girls and 1 boy). Show the children the cards and tell them that each time a card is displayed they are to form groups of that number and gender. Anyone who cannot form the appropriate group misses a turn. At the end comment on the importance of responding to the instructions on the cards.

Today's true story from the Bible is about different responses to God's word. Come back and tell me what those responses were.

CONSOLIDATION 1

Prepare 4 areas:

- path - cardboard or similar laid flat on floor
- rocky places - chairs folded up and laid over each other randomly
- thorns - same as rocky places, but under a sheet or parachute to show choking
- good soil – on a blanket

Broadcast the seed (split peas) onto the 4 places in clear sight of everyone. Divide the children into 4 groups and allocate each group to a different area. Give the children cups to collect the seed. Designate some leaders to be birds to clear as much seed as possible from the path. Once the children have finished collecting the seed see which group has collected the most. Check the 4 areas to see how much seed is left.

WIND-UP 1

Talk about where each group collected seed in the game. What happened to the seed in the story? Comment on how much more seed was collected from the blanket. Discuss the meaning of the parable. God's word is precious and we need to do what it says, just like we needed to obey the instructions on the cards in the warm-up.

WARM-UP 2

The leader acts as a Sergeant-Major and drills the troops. Form the children into ranks and march them around the room. Suggested commands: march forwards, march backwards, mark time, left turn, right turn.

Comment on how well they have done. Would they have got the same result if everyone had done their own thing rather than listening to the leader's commands? Today's true story from the Bible is about the importance of putting God's word into practice.

CONSOLIDATION 2

The children move around to music. Each time the music stops the children decide which of 4 categories they are and do the appropriate actions:

- good soil – stretching up with arms raised
- thorns – crouched on hands and knees
- rocks – rolled in a ball
- path – lying flat.

A leader who has his back turned to the action calls out one group, which is out. Repeat until 3 children are left.

WIND-UP 2

Refer to the categories in the game and recap on the detail of the parable. Remind the children about the warm-up and the importance of doing what the leader said. God's word is precious and should be obeyed.

THE WEEDS

Text: Matthew 13:24-30,36-40

Teaching Point: Good and evil coexist in the world and will do so until Jesus comes again in judgment.

WARM-UP 1

The leader makes a milk shake using milk, cocoa powder, nutmeg, vanilla, cinnamon, 2 fresh eggs, 2 hard boiled eggs and a milk shake maker. Add the ingredients, leaving the eggs until last. Take a fresh egg and break it into the container. Take one of the hard boiled eggs and crack it over the container. It will not break easily. Shell the egg to show that it is hard boiled. Point out how hard it was to tell that from the outside. Take the remaining 2 eggs and ask one or two of the children to identify the fresh egg. Make sure the hard boiled egg is chosen and break it over the container. Shell the egg to show it is hard boiled. Repeat how hard it is to tell the difference. Crack the remaining egg (fresh) into the container.

Today's true story from the Bible is about 2 things that were so alike that it was hard to tell the difference between the two. Come back and tell me:

1. What were the 2 things?

2. What happened to each of them?

NB: Do not allow the children to drink any of the mixture containing raw egg.

CONSOLIDATION 1

A gathering and sorting game, using a selection of coloured sponges, coloured paper, etc. Deposit all the items in the centre of the room. Divide the children into teams and place the teams at points around the edge of the room. The leader calls out a number of items to collect, such as 5 yellow, or 3 red, or 6 sponges, 8 blue triangles, etc. The first child of each team races into the centre and picks up one of the specified items. On return to base the second child runs to collect one item. Continue until the required number of items have been collected. Points are awarded each time for the first team to collect the items. All the items are returned to the centre and the game continues. Make sure that some items are harder to distinguish than others, e.g. green triangles, green circles and green squares.

WIND-UP 1

Refer to the game and the importance of being able to distinguish one thing from another. This was simple when the items collected were easily distinguishable, but not so easy when there were other similar items present. Remind the children of the warm-up and how impossible it was to distinguish the hard boiled from the fresh egg. Go over the answers to the questions from the warm-up.

WARM-UP 2

Prior to the session take 2 different newspapers, one tabloid and one broadsheet, tear them into strips and jumble them up. Place the jumbled up strips in a pile and ask the children to divide them into their separate piles.

Today's true story from the Bible is about 2 things that were very difficult to separate. Come back and tell me:

1. What were the 2 things?

2. What happened to each of them?

CONSOLIDATION 2

Divide the children into teams and give each team a sorting tray. Hide small cups of mixed cereals around the room, enough for each team to collect 6 cups. The cups should be colour coded so that each team can distinguish their own cups. The teams have to find their 6 cups of mixed cereals, bring them back to base and sort them into individual piles. The first team to complete the task successfully is the winner.

WIND-UP 2

Discuss the difficulty of sorting similar items one from the other with reference to the warm-up and game. Recap on the details of the parable.

THE HIDDEN TREASURE AND THE PEARL

Text: Matthew 13:44-46

Teaching Point: Belonging to God's kingdom is worth any sacrifice.

WARM-UP 1

Leader 1 gives a general introduction to the day's programme. Leader 2 interrupts with, 'I've just heard that (name of absent leader) is ill and needs some medicine urgently. It will cost £2.00. Can you help?'

Leader 1 looks in his pockets and brings out £10.00 in coins. He counts out the coins and works out that he can manage to spare £2.00 (I need x for my bus fare, x for my lunch, etc). Leader 1 gives £2.00 to Leader 2, who exits.

Leader 1 continues with the introduction and is interrupted by Leader 3 with, 'I've just heard that x is ill.' Leader 1 says he knows that. He has just given Leader 2 £2.00 for the medicine. Leader 3 says that x is worse than they thought and the medicine will cost £5.00. Can Leader 1 manage another £3.00?

Leader 1 counts out his money and works out that, if he walks home and does without something, he could manage another £3.00. After all, he still has £5.00 left. Leader 3 takes the money and exits.

Leader 1 continues with the introduction and is interrupted by Leader 2 with, 'I'm awfully sorry, but the medicine will cost £10.00.' Leader 1 agonises over whether he can spare the extra £5.00. It is all that he has. Eventually Leader 1 gives Leader 2 the rest of his money and Leader 2 exits.

Today's true story from the Bible is about 2 men who found something precious. Come back and tell me:

1. What did they find?

2. How much did they give for it?

CONSOLIDATION 1

Divide the children into teams and give each team 20 tokens. Prepare 15 boxes, each box containing a number of tokens, the number varying from box to box. Tell the children that they are at an auction. Each of the 15 boxes contains some tokens. The boxes will be displayed one at a time and the teams will use their tokens to bid for the box. The team that proffers the highest bid wins that box. When a team wins a box the box is opened and the contents are added to that team's tokens. Team members have to agree on the number of tokens to bid each time. The winner is the team that amasses the highest number of tokens after all 15 boxes have been auctioned.

WIND-UP 1

Remind the children of the warm-up and go over the questions. Refer to the game and talk about the number of tokens teams were prepared to bid. God's kingdom is not like the auction where the teams did not know what the boxes contained. Jesus said that belonging to God's kingdom is worth any sacrifice.

THE HIDDEN TREASURE AND THE PEARL

Text: Matthew 13:44-46

Teaching Point: Belonging to God's kingdom is worth any sacrifice.

WARM-UP 2

Show the children a selection of containers with items inside of different value. Hold up the containers one at a time and ask the children to state whether they think the contents are valuable or not valuable. Show them the contents. Did they get it right?

Suggested items: chocolate biscuit, dried peas, earring, money, etc.

Today's true story from the Bible is about a man who found some treasure where he was not expecting it. Come back and tell me:

1. Where was the treasure hidden?

2. What did the man have to do to get it?

CONSOLIDATION 2

Place a selection of items on a table, some desirable, some not, such as a tin of baked beans, an apple, an old trainer, a smelly sock, a pencil. In the centre place a large box of sweets. Label each item with a numbered tariff. Hide tokens around the room. Tell the children that tokens are hidden around the room for them to find. When they have collected sufficient tokens these can be exchanged for an item on the table. (The items are not to keep.) E.g. if a pencil is labelled '5' it can be obtained by paying the leader 5 tokens. The large box of sweets is worth the total number of tokens. Encourage the children to work out that they need to work together and give up all their tokens for the sweets.

WIND-UP 2

Remind the children of the warm-up and go over the questions. Refer to the game. If they did not collect the sweets point out what they missed by not being prepared to give up everything. If they did collect the sweets point out what they gained by giving up everything and share out the sweets.

THE TRUSTED KING

Text: Matthew 14:22-33

Teaching Point: We need to trust God regardless of circumstances.

WARM-UP 1

Use Hangman to elicit the word 'Trust'. Explain what 'trust' means for the younger ones.

Enter 2 or 3 leaders dressed as characters in fancy hats or jackets. Each character is asked why he acts as he does. They give different answers, such as, 'Because I like being the centre of attention.' 'Because I like pleasing people.' 'Because I always drop things'. 'Because I act without thinking.'

After each answer the leader asks the children if they would trust that person to ....? It's sometimes hard to trust people. Today's true story from the Bible is about someone who found it hard to trust. Come back and tell me:

1. What was the person's name?

2. What difficult situation was he in?

3. How did he show that he trusted?

CONSOLIDATION 1

A re-enactment of the story. You need a blue sheet, a toy boat and some play people. Place the sheet on the floor with the children sitting round the outside. As the storm comes up the children take hold of the sheet and shake it gently to make waves. Older children work Jesus and Peter.

Play a game with the children holding the sheet at waist height. Place some paper boats at one side of the sheet and see how long it takes to get the boats from one side to the other by moving the sheet. Any boats that fall off go back to the centre. If space permits use 2 sheets and play one against the other. If space is limited divide

the children into 2 teams and time each team one after the other. The winner is the team to get their boats across the lake (sheet) in the shortest time.

WIND-UP 1

Talk about how Peter found it hard to trust Jesus when he looked at his circumstances. Ask the children to suggest difficult circumstances or scary things, such as exams, night time, being left, teasing. Reassure them that we can always trust Jesus, he is not like the characters in the warm-up.

21

THE TRUSTED KING

Text: Matthew 14:22-33

Teaching Point: We need to trust God regardless of circumstances.

Memory verse: *Trust in the Lord with all your heart. Proverbs 3:5*

WARM-UP 2

Place a series of statements on the board (see below).

Tell the children that some of these statements are about the person in today's Bible story. Ask them to say which they think are true and which are false. If they think they know who the person is they are not to shout out the name.

Label the board at the top with 'True' and 'False'. Pin each statement in the correct column as directed by the children.

Statements:

Had a brother	Loved bananas
Lived in an igloo	Had a wife
Had 3 legs	Trusted Jesus
Lived at Capernaum	A tax collector
A fisherman	Lived at Jerusalem
One of Jesus' disciples	Had a pet llama

Recap on what they think, e.g. so you think in today's true story from the Bible you will meet a 3 legged tax-collector who loves bananas. Let's see if you are right. Come back and tell me:

1. The name of the person

2. What did that person learn about Jesus?

CONSOLIDATION 2

A team game to collect the 9 words of the memory verse. Divide the children into teams of not more than 9. Prepare one set of memory verse words for each team. If wished you could include some bogus words to make it more of a challenge. Place the memory verse sets at one end of the room and the children start at the other. Each team requires a boat (a plastic sledge, a large cardboard box, a crate, a mat or a blanket). The older children pull or push the boat across the lake whilst the smaller children ride. When the boat reaches the far side of the lake the rider picks up 1 piece of memory verse and the boat returns to the start. The winner is the first team to collect their words and form them into the memory verse.

WIND-UP 2

Go over the questions. Go over the statements and change them as necessary. Talk about the statement 'Trusted Jesus'. Recap on the story and decide whether Peter did or did not trust Jesus. Reinforce that we can always trust Jesus because he is God. The more Peter knew Jesus the more he knew he could trust him. Revise the memory verse.

FORGIVENESS IN PRAYER

Text: Matthew 18:19-35

Teaching Point: God expects us to forgive others in the same way that he has forgiven us.

WARM-UP 1

Leader 1 shows the children a painting and explains that this is a family heirloom. He calls his servant (Leader 2) and tells him to put it up on the wall. The servant decides he needs a helper and calls Leader 3 to help. As they try to fix it with blue-tak to an upended table the servant drops the painting and puts his foot through it. Leader 1 comes in and sees what has happened. He is very angry and the servant pleads for forgiveness. Leader 1 eventually forgives his servant and exits. The servant turns on his helper and blames him for everything, including some other catastrophes. The servant storms out, followed by the helper pleading, 'I didn't mean it.'

Leader 1 comments that that was not a good way to behave, was it? In today's true story from the Bible something similar happens. Listen carefully and come back and tell me if the servant was right to behave as he did.

CONSOLIDATION 1

Divide the children into teams and hold an egg and spoon relay race, using table tennis balls instead of eggs. Leaders 2 and 3 join in on different teams. Leader 2 cheats outrageously by holding the ball on the spoon with his other hand. Leader 1 calls a halt to the game and chastises Leader 2, who says sorry. Leader 2 is forgiven and allowed to continue. Leader 3 cheats in a small way by occasionally steadying the ball on the spoon. Leader 2 insists that the game is stopped and is unwilling to let Leader 3 rejoin the game. If you want to continue the game ban both and say, 'I'll deal with you two later.'

WIND-UP 1

Invite the 2 servants back and interview them about what happened using game and/or warm-up scenarios. Ask the children what should happen to the unforgiving servant. Talk about the importance of forgiving other people who wrong us. Make sure that they know that this is not an easy thing to do.

WARM-UP 2

An object lesson on forgiveness. Prepare a collection of boxes or bricks labelled with various sins. Leader 2 picks up a box and tells the children that he has sinned / done something wrong. What he did is written on the label on the box. Leader 2 asks the children what he should do about it? Should he ask for forgiveness? He does so and Leader 1 takes the box and places it in a large sack or pillow case. Repeat until all the boxes have been dealt with.

Leader 1 asks the children if they know what God does with forgiven sins? Does he keep them so that he always knows what you did wrong? Leader 1 takes a box out of the sack and reads out the label. No. He puts them somewhere where no one ever remembers them. Leader 1 replaces the box in the sack. They are gone forever. Isn't that wonderful? The Bible tells us that God does not remember our sins any more.

In today's true story from the Bible we will find out what God expects from us as a result.

CONSOLIDATION 2

A chase game. Mark off an area to be the sin bin. Designate several leaders as catchers. The children run around and, when tagged, drop to their knees and beg for mercy. The catchers decide whether or not to grant mercy. If mercy is granted the child carries on. If mercy is not granted the child goes to the sin bin. When everyone has been caught they all need to beg for mercy. Leader 1 forgives them and the game restarts.

The catchers must be leaders because the decision as to whether the child has begged hard enough for mercy might be a difficult one.

WIND-UP 2

Recap on the obligations for forgiveness, using a small bag of marbles to represent the small things we need to forgive and the sack from the warm-up to represent the big things God has forgiven us.

THE RICH YOUNG MAN

Text: Matthew 19:16-22

Teaching Point: Things can get in the way of following Jesus.

WARM-UP 1

Leader 1 is trying to do something, such as undoing a knot or threading a needle. Leader 2 gets in the way. Leader 1 gives up, places a chorus or the memory verse on the OHP and starts to read it out. Leader 2 gets in the way so that the words are not visible on the screen. Leader 1 tries to tell the children something about the programme. Leader 2 starts singing and crashing around so that Leader 1 cannot be heard.

Leader 1 turns to Leader 2 and says, 'Whatever I try to do, you get in the way.' Leader 2 says, 'That's because today's true story from the Bible is about something getting in the way.' Leader 1 sends the children to their groups. Come back and tell me:

1. Who was the man in the story?
2. What got in his way?
3. What did it stop him from doing?

CONSOLIDATION 1

Hide tokens around the room, at least one for each child. The children find a token and take it to the leader, who exchanges it for a wrapped sweet or raisins. The children are told they are not allowed to eat the sweet. Once a child has got his sweet he helps other children find their tokens.

When all the children have found their tokens and exchanged them for sweets the leader holds out a box and asks them to give them up. Those children who give up their sweets go to one side of the leader. Those children who have eaten their sweets or who are unwilling to give them up go to the opposite side. (If there are none of the latter some leaders are primed to take on that role.)

WIND-UP 1

Contrast the 2 groups. Remind the children of the warm-up and go over the questions. Talk about how hard it was for the young man to give up his money and how hard it was for them to give up their sweets. Before finishing, share the sweets in the box with the group that gave them up.

WARM-UP 2

Leader 1 asks Leader 2 what is the most important thing in his life. Leader 2 responds, 'The most important thing in my life is … (football, fishing, fitness, cars, collecting, etc.).' Leader 1 interviews Leader 2 about his hobby. Leader 2 talks about his hobby in great detail. Eventually Leader 1 confronts Leader 2 with his obsession. How much time does he spend each week on it? How much money does he spend each week on it? Bring out the fact that the hobby gets in the way of doing other important things like family, church and friendships.

Today's true story from the Bible is about a man who also had something getting in the way of more important things. Come back and tell me:

1. Who was the man in the story?
2. What got in his way?
3. What did it stop him from doing?

CONSOLIDATION 2

Divide the children into teams and run a relay race over an obstacle course. Use tables and chairs as the obstacles, some covered by sheets to make tunnels, and label each obstacle with one of the following:

sport/fame	power
friends	toys
family	pets
money	career/exams
music/TV	video games
hobbies	food/sweets

The first team to finish wins.

WIND-UP 2

Go up to the obstacles one at a time. Is Jesus more important than this? Explain that each one is all right as long as it doesn't get in the way of following Jesus. Give or elicit appropriate examples. Dismantle each obstacle as you talk about it. Remind the children of the warm-up and how easy it is to let things get in the way.

THE LABOURERS

Text: Matthew 20:1-16

Teaching Point: God gives eternal life to all his servants, regardless of merit or length of service.

WARM-UP 1

Ask for volunteers and give each one a task to perform, some more difficult than others. Give each volunteer the same reward, regardless of the task performed.

Suggested tasks: arm wrestle a leader, pick up rubbish and place in a bin, balance a small object on the nose, build a tower of 10 cups or bricks, shake the leader's hand, tap 3 times on a table/wall, curtsey.

Ask the children if they think you are fair? Let's see if you are right. Today's true story from the Bible is about some people who worked for a reward. Come back and tell me:

1. What work did the people do?

2. What reward did each one receive?

CONSOLIDATION 1

Give the children a stack of newspaper, sticky tape, a blanket or sheet, pens and scissors and ask them to make a vineyard. They can also use their bodies. Encourage them to make a wall, vines, an entrance, a path, a winepress, a watchtower, etc. This can be done as a whole group activity or in teams, depending on the size of the group. If operating in teams, give each group a leader and a set of written instructions. Inspect the vineyards at the end and give the children a reward.

WIND-UP 1

Refer to the game and discuss what a vineyard looks like and what happens there. Go over the details of the parable. Refer to the warm-up. Go over the questions. Were they right when they decided whether or not Leader 1 acted fairly?

WARM-UP 2

Call a big child out to the front and ask him to run on the spot, then do 4 star jumps. Choose another child to join him and repeat the exercise. Repeat until 5 children are up front. Encourage the first children to keep going if they start to flag. Once the fifth child has joined the line bring the exercise session to a halt after 30 seconds. Place 20 tokens on the table and ask the whole group how the 5 children should be rewarded with tokens. Place the tokens in appropriate piles and say that the rewards will be handed out at the end of the session.

In today's true story from the Bible some people were given rewards. Let's see if they were given as you suggest. Come back and tell me:

1. What work did the people do?

2. What reward did each one receive?

CONSOLIDATION 2

Divide the children into small groups. Give each group a piece of paper on which is written an activity to mime. All the activities take place in a vineyard.

Suggested activities: picking grapes, treading grapes, eating lunch, weeding, digging, planting vines, repairing walls, pruning, making wine.

The groups take it in turns to mime their activity to the rest, who have to guess what the activity is.

WIND-UP 2

Refer to the game and discuss what a vineyard looks like and what happens there. Go over the details of the parable. Refer to the warm-up. Go over the questions. Were they right when they decided whether or not the Leader acted fairly?

Lesson 13 and Lesson 18

Tokens

Picture Pairs

THE TWO SONS

Text: Matthew 21:23-32

Teaching Point: Faith without works is dead.

WARM-UP 1

Ask for 2 volunteers from the children, 1 to be blindfolded and 1 to give instructions. Place several items that make a noise when stepped on as a obstacle course. Suggested items: moulded plastic trays, cornflakes between sheets of newspaper, popadoms. The blindfolded child starts at one end of the course and is directed by the other child to walk through the course without stepping on any of the obstacles.

A leader helps the child giving instructions, so that blindfolded child completes the course successfully .

Then an adult volunteer is blindfolded and directed through the course by one of the leaders. The adult makes a big point of saying that he will listen. He tests his ears, fusses that the blindfold will stop them hearing, will the leader's voice be loud enough, etc. Then the adult disregards the instructions and steps on all the obstacles. The leader takes him to task, saying that he did not listen to the instructions. The adult volunteer says that he did **say** he would listen. The leader states that saying and doing are 2 different things.

Which one listened and obeyed?

In today's true story from the Bible we will find out what happened when someone promised to do something. Come back and tell me:

1. Who were the 2 men in the story?

2. What were they asked to do?

3. What was their response?

CONSOLIDATION 1

Prepare a series of tasks for the children to do, some which are achievable and some which are not. Suggested tasks: carry a tray containing table tennis balls from one end of the room to the other without any falling off, throw table tennis balls into a bucket, do 25 press ups, do 50 star jumps, do not blink for 30 seconds, estimate a minute, lie on the floor for 2 minutes without moving or making a noise, etc. Ask the children, 'Who thinks they can ....?' All those who think they can, come out and attempt the task.

WIND-UP 1

Refer to the game and make the point that it is no good saying you can do something if you cannot. Saying something and doing it are 2 different things. Words are no good by themselves. Refer back to the warm-up. Which volunteer listened and obeyed? Jesus told the Bible story to people who said that they loved God, but their actions showed that they did not really love him. Jesus wants us to know that saying we are Christians / God's friends is not enough on its own. If we really love Jesus we must do what he says.

THE TWO SONS

Text: Matthew 21:23-32

Teaching Point: Faith without works is dead.

Memory verse: *Faith without actions is dead. James 2:26*

WARM-UP 2

A leader comes in dressed as a slimy salesman and promises to do a lot of wonderful things for the Sunday school and its leaders, such as redecorate the building, scrub the tables, provide chocolate biscuits every week, do all the cutting out for the leaders, make visual aids for all the classes, etc. Other leaders ask him if he will also do special things for them, such as clean the car, do the ironing, walk the dog, etc. The slimy salesman says he will do everything.

Ask the children if they believe him? In today's true story from the Bible we will find out what happened when someone promised to do something. Come back and tell me:

1. Who were the 2 men in the story?
2. What were they asked to do?
3. What was their response?

CONSOLIDATION 2

A memory verse game. Prepare sets of the memory verse plus reference with one word written on each sheet of paper, giving a set of 6 sheets of paper.

Place enough chairs for all the children in rows of 6 around the room (see diagram for 24 children). Place the memory verse sheets face down in the centre. The children choose any chair to sit on. On command the children run into the centre, pick up a word and decide where to sit. They can sit in any row of chairs, but must sit in the appropriate chair in that row so that the words in the row make up the memory verse. E.g. a child who picks up 'actions' will sit in the third chair from the left. Once all the children are seated they hold up their sheets of paper to see if they have got it right. The leader corrects as necessary. Have a dummy run to start with.

If there are a large number of younger children they will find it easier if the sets are colour coded and rows of chairs are colour designated, i.e. the blue sheets of paper go to the blue row of chairs.

A variation is for one child from each row to go at a time. On command the child on the left of each row runs into the centre, picks up a word and sits on the appropriate chair, turfing off the person sitting on it, who runs into the centre for a word. Children do not have to return to the same row.

WIND-UP 2

Refer back to the warm-up. Do they think the slimey salesperson would do what he said? Saying something and doing it are 2 different things. Words are no good by themselves. Jesus told the Bible story to people who said that they loved God, but their actions showed that they did not really love him. Jesus wants us to know that saying we are Christians / God's friends is not enough on its own. If we really love Jesus we must do what he says. Revise the memory verse.

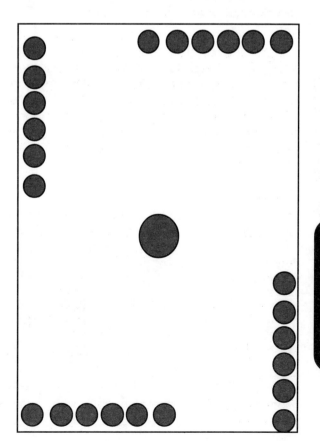

THE TENANTS

Text: Matthew 21:33-46

Teaching Point: God's kingdom is for those who accept his son as Lord and Saviour.

Memory verse: *Faith without actions is dead. James 2:26.*

WARM-UP 1

Leader 2 builds a tower in a reckless manner, using either large objects such as chairs or small ones such as plastic cups and bricks. Leader 1 keeps warning leader 2, 'If you do it that way it will fall down.' Ask the children if they think that the warnings are true? The tower falls over and leader 2 is very upset. In today's true story from the Bible we have a story Jesus told as a warning to the hearers.

1. Who were the hearers?
2. In the story, who did the master send to his tenants?
3. What did the tenants do to the last messenger?
4. What was the warning?

CONSOLIDATION 1

Pick the grapes. Divide the children into teams of no more than 8 players. Each team has a set of 8 balloons (grapes) in a crate, bin bag or similar. Prior to the lesson blow up the balloons and insert a rolled up strip of paper containing one word of the memory verse into each one. Tell the children that the start area is their winepress.

The children run one at a time to the crate, pick a balloon and run back to the winepress. There they jump on the balloon (press the grape) to burst it and collect the contents (1 word of the memory verse). Once the child has returned to the winepress with the grape, the next child goes. The winning team is the first one to collect all their words and glue them onto a piece of paper in the correct order.

WIND-UP 1

Remind the children about the religious authorities. What did Jesus say would happen to them? Remind them what happened when the warning in the warm-up was neglected.

Jesus taught that if we reject him, he will reject us when he comes again to take all his people to heaven.

WARM-UP 2

Exhibit symbols of the elements of wine making, such as leaves, grapes, winepress, separator, bottle, cork, glass, grape seeds. Display the articles one at a time and ask the children if they know what they have in common.

Today's true story from the Bible is about growing grapes and running a vineyard. Come back and tell me if it was a well run vineyard or a badly run one and why Jesus told this story.

CONSOLIDATION 2

Prior to the lesson make lots of grapes from playdough. Hide them around the area. Divide the children into teams. The children search for the grapes and take them back to their home base where they squash the grapes and make a big ball from the playdough. Weigh the balls to determine the winner.

This is a good story to act out as a way of reinforcing the story detail.

Playdough Recipe

Ingredients:
2 cups plain flour
2 cups water
1 cup salt
2 dessert spoons cooking oil
2 oz cream of tartar
food colouring

Mix all the ingredients together in a large saucepan and cook over a low heat, stirring constantly, until the mixture forms a stiff dough. This takes 5 -10 minutes. Turn the dough out onto a board or work top and knead until the dough is easily malleable. Wrap the dough in cling film and leave to cool. Periodically take the dough out of the cling film and knead to remove the crust that forms as it cools. Once the dough is cold give it a final knead and replace in fresh cling film. The dough can be stored wrapped in cling film in an airtight container, e.g. ice cream container, for up to 6 months.

WIND-UP 2

Go over the answers to the questions from the warm-up. Discuss why Jesus told this story. Remind the children of what happened to the original tenants. Jesus taught that if we reject him, he will reject us when he comes again to take all his people to heaven.

THE TEN GIRLS

Text: Matthew 25:1-13

Teaching Point: Being ready for Jesus' return.

WARM-UP 1

Prior to the lesson hide a Bible, a teacher's lesson book, some craft work and craft equipment around the room. At the start of the warm-up place a large box on the table and start to pull things out and scatter them around the table and floor. Items in the box can include clothing, books, toys, etc. Explain to the children that you woke up late and have not had time to get your things ready for the morning. Meanwhile keep pulling things out of the box, commenting on the items as you do so. Eventually tell the children what you are missing and ask them to help you find them. As the children find the missing items set them out on the table at the front.

Point out that you were totally unprepared for the lesson. Was this a good thing to be? Today's true story from the Bible is a story Jesus told about the importance of being ready. Come back and tell me:

1. Who was the story about?

2. How many of them were ready and what for?

While the game is in progress a leader approaches the bus stop from the other end of the room and leads off any children standing there to a separate area. (Prime a leader to remain at the bus stop in case all the children join the game.)

Draw the game to a close and point out that the children at the bus stop have gone. When the 'bus' came those playing the game were not ready, so got left behind.

CONSOLIDATION 1

Bus stop game: Designate a spot to be the bus stop and mark it with a chair or similar. Line up the children at the bus stop and tell them that you are expecting a bus to come to take them to a party. Ask the children to watch for the bus. Can they see anyone coming? Comment on how long they are waiting. After a short time suggest that you could play a game to pass away the time. Play a relay race or other game that the children enjoy. Encourage the children to join in.

WIND-UP 1

Remind the children of the warm-up and go over the answers to the questions. Point out that the 5 maidens who were not ready were left behind, just like in the game. Ensure that the children understand that Jesus told this story to warn his people to be ready for his return, so that they would be with him in heaven forever.

THE TEN GIRLS

Text: Matthew 25:1-13

Teaching Point: Being ready for Jesus' return.

WARM-UP 2

Explain to the children that they need to get ready for your inspection. Once they are in rows put them through their paces as follows, with the leader demonstrating the action to be followed. Once the action has been completed the children can be inspected to see if they are ready.

- Army - stand still in lines with feet together and arms at sides.
- Airforce - stand in rows with arms outstretched and sufficient space between each child for fingers not to touch.
- Ready for bed - clean teeth and lie on the floor.
- Ready for a meal - sit cross-legged on the floor with hands held out to check cleanliness.
- Ready for a journey - pack bag and walk to one side of the room.

Comment on the importance of being ready for the various activities. Today's true story from the Bible is a story Jesus told about the importance of being ready. Come back and tell me:

1. Who was the story about?
2. How many of them were ready and what for?

CONSOLIDATION 2

Divide the children into teams, each with a leader or older child. For each team prepare a set of 10 containers with lids, some containing written instructions and some empty (see opposite). Write 'R' (for ready) on the base of 5 of the containers. Place the containers in a marked area of the room equidistant from the team bases. Using mats or pieces of newspaper, make a line of stepping stones from each team base to the containers. The team members take it in turns to run along the stepping stones, pick up a container and return to base, where the container is opened and the instruction inside

read out and obeyed. (If collecting containers from another team show that team the instruction.) The next team member does not run until the instruction has been completed. All instruction slips are retained by the team leader and any breach of the rules results in a box being returned to the main pile. The first team to collect 10 boxes wins.

Instructions for the containers:

- Return 2 containers to the centre.
- Collect 1 box from the team on your left.
- Give 1 box to the team on your left.
- Everyone do 5 push ups.
- Everyone lie on the ground and count to 30 seconds.
- Take a free box from the centre.
- Take 2 boxes from any other team.
- Return 1 box to the centre.
- Put all your boxes in the centre and start again.

WIND-UP 2

Ask the children why they collected 10 boxes - what is the significance of the number 10. Turn over the containers and count how many have 'R' on the base. What does 'R' stand for? Remind the children of the warm-up and go over the answers to the questions. Point out that the 5 maidens who were not ready were left behind. Ensure that the children understand that Jesus told this story to warn his people to be ready for his return so, that they would be with him in heaven forever.

THE THREE SERVANTS

Text: Matthew 25:14-30

Teaching Point: We need to use the opportunities and abilities God has given us to serve him.

WARM-UP 1

Ask for 3 volunteers from the children to take part in a quiz show and sit them on chairs at the front. Explain that you are the quizmaster and you will ask them questions one at a time. A correct answer doubles their points, whereas a wrong answer puts them out of the game. If they do not know the answer they can pass. Any question that has been passed on is offered to the next player. The starter question for each player is for 5 points. Questions can be based on previous lessons or on general knowledge.

At the end of the quiz comment on how well the contestants did, starting with nothing and building it up. Today's true story from the Bible is about some people who were given something to start with. Come back and tell me:

1. How many people were given something?

2. What was each one given and what did he do with it?

3. What happened to each of them as a result?

CONSOLIDATION 1

Tell the children that they are waiters in a restaurant and the owner is coming to inspect it. They need to set up some tables and chairs and lay the tables for the customers. Provide tablecloths, serviettes, cutlery, etc. Appoint one or two older children to be chief waiters to supervise the others. One or two leaders and those children who do not wish to take part can sit and watch. When the restaurant is ready a leader inspects it, commending the children for their hard work.

WIND-UP 1

Remind the children about the warm-up and how well the contestants did. Review the answers to the questions. Comment on the game and the fact that only the children who took part were commended. Point out that everyone can help to get ready for Jesus' return. Discuss how we do this - love God, love parents, do good to others, tell others about Jesus.

THE THREE SERVANTS

Text: Matthew 25:14-30

Teaching Point: We need to use the opportunities and abilities God has given us
                     to serve him.

WARM-UP 2

Skit or puppets (see script on page 72). Leader explains that he has been visiting some friends. They have 2 children, Toby and Trudy. He is just about to leave and calls Toby and Trudy to say goodbye. He wants to give them a present. Each one gets 10 coins and is told to use them wisely. The leader says goodbye and goes away. Toby and Trudy spend some time discussing how they will spend their money. Trudy decides to spend hers on sweets, whereas Toby puts some away for holidays and to buy presents, leaving just 1 coin to buy sweets. Matilda arrives asking to be sponsored to run around the school playground in order to earn money for a new science laboratory. The sponsorship will amount to 1 coin. Toby agrees to sponsor Matilda and go without his sweets. Trudy spends all her 10 coins on sweets.

The leader asks the children which puppet did the right thing with the money he gave them? Toby or Trudy? Today's true story from the Bible is a story Jesus told to his friends. I want you to come back and tell me what the people were given and what they did with it.

CONSOLIDATION 2

Divide the children into teams and give each team 5 red tokens, 5 blue ones, 5 green ones and 5 yellow ones. Place a box containing 2 tokens of each colour equidistant from the team bases. Explain that the aim of the game is to collect 10 tokens of one colour. Give the teams a short period of time to decide which colour they want to collect. On the signal to start the first player from each team runs to the box and deposits an unwanted token, exchanging it for one of the desired colour. On return to the team base the second player repeats the process. Continue until 10 tokens of one colour have been collected. Teams are allowed to change the colour they are collecting at any point in the game.

WIND-UP 2

Remind the children of the warm-up and which puppet did the right thing with the money they were given. Go over the answers to the questions. Comment on how hard the children had to work in the game to collect 10 tokens. Point out that Jesus expects all his friends to work hard serving him while they wait for his return. Discuss how we do this - love God, love parents, do good to others, tell others about Jesus.

THE BETRAYED KING

Text: Matthew 26:31-58,69-75

Teaching Point: We need to watch and pray if we are not to fall into temptation.

WARM-UP 1

Ask the children to do whatever you do. Tell them that you will not speak so they need to watch very carefully. Perform a variety of actions with the children copying them. When you have finished produce 1 cup, trophy or similar for each class group and hand them out. Tell them that they are to keep alert and guard their trophy for the rest of the session.

In today's true story from the Bible Jesus told some men to keep alert and pray. Come back and tell me:

1. The names of the men.

2. Why did Jesus tell them to watch and pray?

3. What did one of the men do at the end of the story?

CONSOLIDATION 1

The children stand in a group in the middle of the room. The leader shouts, 'Betrayal!', closes his eyes and counts out loud to 20. When 'Betrayal!' is shouted the children run and hide. After counting to 20 the leader opens his eyes. Any children visible are deemed caught and are either out or miss 1-2 turns, depending on whether or not you want a winner. Then the leader calls, 'Forgiven!' and the children remaining in the game return to the centre.

Repeat for as many times as desired.

Children holding trophies should keep hold of them during the game. Any trophies left on the side should be confiscated.

WIND-UP 1

Remind the children of the warm-up and check that they still have hold of their trophies. Comment appropriately and go over the answers to the questions. Discuss Peter's betrayal of Jesus and his sorrow at what he had done. Refer to the game and the fact that having run away to hide at the shout of 'Betrayal!' they needed forgiveness to return. Point out that we all do things that make Jesus sad, but God promises that if we are truly sorry he will forgive us (1 John 1:9).

THE BETRAYED KING

Text: Matthew 26:31-58,69-75

Teaching Point: We need to watch and pray if we are not to fall into temptation.

Memory verse: *Trust in the Lord with all your heart. Proverbs 3:5.*

WARM-UP 2

Place a large box on a table at the front and bring out various items one by one. Some items are connected with the story, others not. Items can be models or drawings. Suggested items are

- a nose
- an ear
- a set of lips
- an eye
- a finger
- a sword
- a foot
- a cockrel
- a bow and arrows
- a lamb, etc.

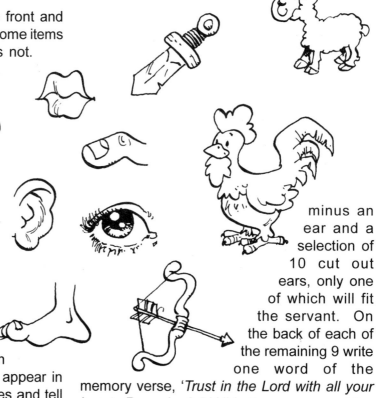

As each item is displayed the children decide whether or not that item will appear in the story. Divide the items into 2 piles and tell the children to come back after the story to find out whether they made the right decisions.

CONSOLIDATION 2

Divide the children into teams. For each team prepare a picture of the High Priest's servant

minus an ear and a selection of 10 cut out ears, only one of which will fit the servant. On the back of each of the remaining 9 write one word of the memory verse, '*Trust in the Lord with all your heart. Proverbs 3:5.*' Hide the ears around the room. Each team collects a set of 10 ears and glues the appropriate ear in place on the picture. The remaining 9 ears are put in order to make the memory verse. Ears can either be colour coded for each team, or the teams can exchange ears one at a time. The winner is the first team to complete the task.

WIND-UP 2

Look at the warm-up items and go over which ones were included in the story. Revise the story details as you go. Refer to the game and revise the memory verse. Point out that it is when we do not trust Jesus with all our heart that we become frightened and fall into temptation, just as Peter did. Was Peter truly sorry? We all do things that make Jesus sad, but God promises that if we are truly sorry he will forgive us (1 John 1:9).

THE CRUCIFIXION

Text: Matthew 27:15-61

Teaching Point: Jesus died in our place.

WARM-UP 1

Use a skit or puppets to show a situation where a child does something wrong and another child is punished for it (see puppet script on page 74). Toby and Trudy are looking forward to Easter and Trudy notices a packet of foil wrapped Easter eggs (or similar). Toby tells her that they are his. Would Trudy like one? Trudy looks in the packet to find that they are all gone. Only the foil wrappings are left. Toby admits to eating them. He suggests Trudy might like some of the foil wrapping to make things with. Trudy takes some foil wrapping. The leader appears and tells the children that he has brought a packet of foil wrapped chocolate eggs (or similar) to give them a treat at the end of the session. Toby and Trudy disappear. The leader looks around and sees the packet. When he finds it is empty he is very angry. He calls for the puppets, who eventually appear. When challenged, Toby denies all knowledge of the Easter eggs, but points out that Trudy has the foil wrappers. Trudy is accused and her denials go unheeded. She is sent to her room and told that she will miss out on a coming treat. Toby looks smug.

A second leader asks the children if the right child was punished? In today's true story from the Bible somebody gets a punishment he does not deserve. Come back and tell me:

1. Who was punished unjustly?

2. How was he punished?

3. Who should have been punished? [Barabbas]

CONSOLIDATION 1

Divide the children into teams. Give each team a selection of items that are imperfect in some way, e.g. dirty, written on. Suggested items are cut-outs of people and animals, soft toys, plastic fruit. Each item has a perfect (clean) twin, which has been hidden around the room. The teams collect the perfect twins of all their items. The perfect items are displayed and the imperfect ones placed in a receptacle. The winner is the first team to complete the task.

WIND-UP 1

Remind the children of the warm-up and go over the answers to the questions. Refer to the game. Point out that all the imperfect items were replaced by perfect ones. What happened to the imperfect ones? Point out that Jesus not only died instead of Barabbas, but also in our place. Jesus was perfect and he died in place of us. In the game we got rid of all the imperfect items, never to be seen again. Jesus takes away all our sins when we ask him to be our Saviour.

THE CRUCIFIXION

Text: Matthew 27:15-61

Teaching Point: Jesus died in our place.

WARM-UP 2

Before the session place a chair in clear view with a label, 'Do not sit on this chair.' Leader 2 comes in and sits on it. Leader 1 is angry with Leader 2 asking him why he sat on the chair, can't he read, etc. Leader 1 states that Leader 2 must be punished. After some deliberation the punishment is set as a custard pie to the face. (Use a paper plate covered with shaving foam or whipped cream.) Leader 2 pleads with leader 1 not to be punished. Leader 2 stands quivering, with eyes closed, waiting for the punishment. After a great big build-up leader 1 places the custard pie on his own face.

Leader 2 asks the children if the right person was punished? In today's true story from the Bible somebody gets a punishment he does not deserve. Come back and tell me:

1. Who was punished unjustly?
2. How was he punished?
3. Who should have been punished? [Barabbas]

CONSOLIDATION 2

Play dodge ball. The leaders stand around the edge of the room with the children moving around in the middle. One leader has a soft sponge or plastic ball and throws it to hit a child below the knees. Any child hit must pay a forfeit, such as 10 push-ups, sit-ups, star jumps, squats, rolling from one mark to another, piggy back for the child, etc. The child nominates a leader to pay the forfeit for them. Once the penalty has been paid the child rejoins the game, helping the leaders to throw the balls. Several balls can be used at the same time.

WIND-UP 2

Remind the children of the warm-up and go over the questions. Refer to the game, pointing out that each time a forfeit was required a leader paid it in place of the child. Point out that Jesus not only died instead of Barabbas, but also in our place.

THE RESURRECTION

Text: Matthew 27:62 - 28:15

Teaching Point: Jesus rose from the dead, just as he foretold.

WARM-UP 1

Place a selection of empty containers on a table in clear view of the children. You may want to place all the items in a large box and take them out one at a time until the box is also empty.

Pick up each item and ask the children what they would expect to find inside. Open the container and say, 'There is nothing here, it is empty.' Repeat the process for all the items. Today's true story from the Bible is about people looking for someone, whom they could not find. Come back and tell me;

    1. Who went looking?

    2. Who could not be found?

    3. Why?

CONSOLIDATION 1

The aim of the game is for the children to search for a small container such as a matchbox, containing a strip of paper on which is written, 'He is not here, he has been raised, just as he said,' (Matthew 28:6) and not find it. Prepare a matchbox with the message in it, a set of 10-12 clues pointing to various locations in the room, and a set of messages, one for each location, all saying, 'it is not here'. If you have limited space you could use a grid board game like 'Battleships' or 'Buried Treasure' to achieve the same end. You also need a container to hold the clues.

Suggested clues: where music is made? (piano), where coats are hung? (coat rack or stand), where tea is made? (kitchen), where you sit to eat? (table), etc. Hide the messages so that they can be found after a short search

but do not make it too easy. Appreciate the age and abilities of the children searching for the messages.

Hide the matchbox on you. Tell the children that they are looking for a matchbox containing an important message. Ask a child to choose a clue from the container. The children work out the location and go there to look for the message. When the message is found the children read it out and return to base. Another child picks a clue and the process is repeated. Continue until there are no clues left. Some children may deduce that they will not find the matchbox, but keep encouraging them to continue looking. The game finishes when there are no clues left.

WIND-UP 1

Remind the children about the warm-up and go over the questions. Refer to the game and ask the children if they became discouraged when they could not find the matchbox with the important message. Refer back to the story when the women first arrived at the tomb and found it empty. How disappointing for them. Produce the matchbox, slowly open it and take out the strip of paper. Remind the children that Jesus wasn't in the tomb because he had risen.

THE RESURRECTION

Text: Matthew 27:62 - 28:15

Teaching Point: Jesus rose from the dead, just as he foretold.

Memory Verse: *'Trust in the Lord with all your heart. Never rely on what you think you know.' Proverbs 3:5*

WARM-UP 2

Prepare a simple map of the country plus some weather symbols, such as suns, cloud, rain, snow, etc., that can be stuck onto it (see visual aids on page 50). Place the map on a board where it can be clearly seen by the children. Explain that you are a weather forecaster and give an improbable forecast, sticking the weather symbols onto the map.

A second leader asks the children if they believe the weather forecaster. Do they think that what he said would happen will happen? In today's true story from the Bible we hear about someone saying that something unlikely would happen. Come back and tell me:

1. What was the unlikely happening?
2. Did the hearers believe it would happen?
3. Did it come true?

CONSOLIDATION 2

Divide the children into teams and ask them to search for as many empty containers as they can find. Some have been hidden beforehand, others may be present in the room anyway. The winning team is the one to collect the most empty containers.

To make the game more challenging each container can be exchanged for one word of the memory verse or for one word from the following statement, 'He is not here, he has been raised, just as he said,' (Matthew 28:6).

WIND-UP 2

Remind the children about the warm-up. Did they believe the weather forecaster? Why not? Go over the answers to the warm-up questions. Comment on the number of empty containers found in the game. Why do they think they were asked to search for empty containers? Jesus was not in the tomb. Go over the message from Matthew 28:6.

JESUS MADE A SICK MAN WELL

Text: Mark 1:40-45

Teaching Point: Jesus could make a sick man well because he is God.

WARM-UP 1

Leader 1 dresses up as a doctor (white coat) and explains that he is a very clever doctor who has made lots of people well. He has some of his instruments with him to show the children. Leader 1 shows the children his instruments. Suggestions are a torch, a small wooden hammer or similar to check reflexes, a stethoscope, bandages and ointments. Leader 1 points out that he has had many years of training to make him a doctor.

Ask for 2 volunteers from the children. They take it in turns to pick a medical condition from the hat (see below) and present themselves to the doctor. The doctor decides what is wrong and prescribes treatment (see below). The doctor tells the patient that his condition will take a while to heal.

Suggested medical conditions are a broken arm (treated with 6 weeks in plaster), influenza (go to bed, drink lots of water and take it carefully), a cut knee (a waterproof plaster) and a verruca (special paint and a sock for swimming).

Today's true story from the Bible is about someone who was ill. Come back and tell me:

1. What was wrong?
2. How did Jesus make him better?
3. How long did it take to make him better?

CONSOLIDATION 1

Divide the children into teams and give each team some broken items to be mended. Can they make them as good as new? Suggestions for broken items are a pencil or piece of wood, a broken box, a magazine that has been pulled apart, a piece of paper or material that has been cut into pieces and a crushed plastic drinks bottle. The teams are handed the first item to be mended and timed. The mended items are inspected and marks allotted. Repeat until all items have been mended. The team with the highest marks wins.

WIND-UP 1

Display the items mended in the game. How well were they done? Could the teams make them as good as new? Remind the children about the warm-up. The doctor could make things better, but could he do it immediately? Go over the answers to the warm-up questions. We cannot make things as good as new and we cannot do it immediately. Jesus can. Why can Jesus do this? Because he is God.

JESUS MADE A SICK MAN WELL

Text: Mark 1:40-45

Teaching Point: Jesus could make a sick man well because he is God.

WARM-UP 2

Ask a real doctor or nurse from the congregation to visit and talk about how they make people well. Show the children some of the things they use. The leader removes those things and asks, 'How would you heal people without these things?'

Today's true story from the Bible is about someone who needed to be made better. Come back and tell me:

1. What was wrong?

2. How did Jesus make him better?

3. What does that show about Jesus?

CONSOLIDATION 2

Divide the children into teams of equal numbers, each with a leader. Prepare a pillow case holding various items that can be identified by touch, one for each team. Use small items such as a sugar cube, lego brick, coin, etc.

Line the teams up with the leaders at a short distance from their teams. Give each leader a pillowcase. Ask the children how clever are their fingers? Tell them the object of the game is to be the first person to find the specified item in the pillowcase without looking inside it. The team members take it in turns to go to their leader and feel inside the pillowcase to find the specified item. The first person to hold it up wins a point for their team. The items are returned to the pillowcase before the next item is specified. Items can be specified more than once. The winner is the team with the highest number of points at the end of the game.

WIND-UP 2

Remind the children of the warm-up and go over the questions. Refer to the game and how clever their fingers are. Point out that lepers lost the feeling in their fingers. Ask 1 or 2 children to put a thick glove on and try to find a specified item in the pillowcase. In Jesus' day leprosy could not be cured. To cure leprosy today takes lots of medicines and a long time. How did Jesus make the man better? Why could Jesus do that? Because he is God.

AUTHORITY OVER SIN

Text: Mark 2:1-12

Teaching Point: Jesus has power to forgive sin because he is God.

Memory Verse: *'Jesus said, "I have been given all authority in heaven and on earth."' Matthew 28:18.*

WARM-UP 1

Leader 1 tells the children that a special guest has agreed to come and tell them what he does. Leader 2 comes in dressed as a football referee (in football kit with a whistle). Leader 1 interviews Leader 2 about his life as a football referee, bringing out the fact that the referee is in charge. Finally Leader 1 asks Leader 2 how can Leader 1 really know if Leader 2 is in control of the players? Leader 2 offers to demonstrate. He asks the children to perform various actions, such as running on the spot, star jumps, etc., and to stop immediately he blows his whistle. After a few minutes of this Leader 1 agrees that Leader 2 has demonstrated that he is in charge.

Today's true story from the Bible is about someone who had authority over something. Come back and tell me:

1. Who was in charge?

2. Over what did he have authority?

3. How do we know that he really did have authority over that thing?

CONSOLIDATION 1

Play Grandmother's Footsteps. Leader 2 (the referee) stands at one end of the room with a whistle, a yellow card and a red card. The children start at the other end of the room. The referee stands with his back to the children. On the command to start the children move at walking pace towards the referee. Periodically the referee turns around, blowing his whistle as he does so. The children must stop immediately. Any child caught moving is shown either a yellow or red card. If shown the yellow card the child cannot move forwards on the next go. If shown the red card the child must return to the start.

WIND-UP 1

Remind the children of the warm-up and go over the answers to the questions. Point out that the referee's authority is only for the length of the game. Refer to the game just played. Jesus' authority is not like that - Jesus' authority is absolute. Point out that in games some players do not like the referee's authority. Who in the Bible story did not like Jesus' authority? [Pharisees and teachers of the Law] Revise the memory verse.

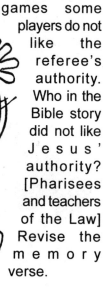

AUTHORITY OVER SIN

Text: Mark 2:1-12

Teaching Point: Jesus has power to forgive sin because he is God.

WARM-UP 2

Who is in charge? Prepare 6 pairs of picture cards to match up, one of each pair having authority over the other. Suggested pairs are teacher and pupil, general and soldier, ship's captain and sailor, king and group of people, football referee and player, plane's captain and steward/stewardess (see visual aids on page 27). Number the cards randomly on the back and pin onto a board face down. The children take it in turns to pick 2 cards by number. These are turned over and, if a pair match they are left face up, if not they are replaced face down. Each time a pair is made ask the children who is in charge of whom? This activity can also be done by forming 2 teams and the teams taking it in turns to choose the numbers.

Discuss what it means to have authority over someone. Today's true story from the Bible is about someone who had authority over something. Come back and tell me:

1. Who was in charge?

2. Over what did he have authority?

3. How do we know that he really did have authority over that thing?

CONSOLIDATION 2

Divide into teams of 5 or 9 children, depending on the size of the children. Each team needs a blanket on which one child can be carried and a safety helmet for that child. The child is carried on the blanket by either 1 child at each corner or by 2 at each corner, depending on the size of the children. Using paper, mark out a slalom course for each team. The team must traverse the course without standing on the paper.

WIND-UP 2

Talk about the game. The child in the blanket could not walk and had to be transported along the course by their friends. This was like the man in the story. What was his most important need - forgiveness or healing? Remind the children of the warm-up and go over the answers to the questions. Why could Jesus forgive sins? Because he is God.

AUTHORITY OVER DISEASE

Text: Mark 3:1-6

Teaching Point: Jesus has power over disease because he is God.

WARM-UP 1

Leader 1 dresses up as a doctor in a white coat and has another leader or child volunteer as a patient. Leader 1 places the patient on the operating table and explains that the patient has a very serious problem that must be operated on. This is a special operation that has never been done before - an operation to remove stubbornness. Where is stubbornness found in the body? Show pictures of various parts of the body, such as heart, liver, brain, kidney, foot, hand, head, stomach, each time asking, 'Is this where we find stubbornness?'. Talk about stubbornness being an attitude - refusing to believe in spite of the evidence.

Today's true story from the Bible is about some people who had stubborn hearts. Come back and tell me:

1. What was wrong with the man in the story?
2. How did Jesus heal him?
3. Who had stubborn hearts?

CONSOLIDATION 1

Divide the children into teams and have a series of events to decide which is the most powerful team. Suggested events are a tug-of-war, and who can lift the heaviest weight? For the weight-lifting exercise use heavy items, such as books, kneelers, chairs, etc., in the middle of a blanket with the team evenly spaced around the edges. Also teams can nominate one member to see who can lift the heaviest carrier bag, using bags of sugar or flour as weight.

WIND-UP 1

Remind the children of the warm-up and go over the answers to the questions. Point out that the people with stubborn hearts refused to listen to and accept Jesus. This made Jesus sad. Refer to the game and which team was the most powerful. Is disease a match for Jesus? Why not? Because he is God.

WARM-UP 2

Place a box on a table in clear view of the children. Bring out wizened or withered items one at a time and ask the children to identify them. Suggested items are wizened fruit and vegetables, withered plants and flowers.

Today's true story from the Bible is about someone who had something that was wizened. Come back and tell me:

1. What was wizened?
2. How did Jesus heal it?
3. Why could Jesus heal it?

CONSOLIDATION 2

Divide the children into teams of at least 2 children. One child from each team attempts the allotted task. After a set period of time a second child helps the first child to complete the task. The children are only allowed to use their left hands. Points can be given for the first team to complete each task.

Suggested tasks are:

- peel a banana
- take off a shoe and sock and replace it
- build a tower with building blocks such as lego bricks
- make a ball out of playdough or clay (see recipe on page 30)
- tear a circle out of a piece of paper
- roll up a sheet of newspaper
- paper folding
- threading cotton reels or similar onto a piece of string.

WIND-UP 2

The man in today's Bible story had a major problem. What was it? Remind the children of the wizened and withered items from the warm-up. Refer to the game and how difficult it was to do things with only one hand. Go over the answers to the warm-up questions. Why could Jesus make him better? Because he is God.

AUTHORITY OVER NATURE

Text: Mark 4:35-41

Teaching Point: Jesus has power over nature because he is God.

Memory verse: *Jesus said, "I have been given all authority in heaven and on earth." Matthew 28:18.*

WARM-UP 1

Use puppets or a skit (see script on page 76).

Leader introduces 2 friends who have come to visit - Toby and Trudy. They talk about what happens in Sunday School and how pleased they are to be there. Toby says how much he enjoys stories, then tells the children a story he heard at school. The story is about a Viking called King Canute who thought he was so powerful that he could stop the tide coming in. The puppets end by agreeing that no-one can tell the sea what to do.

Today's true story from the Bible is about the sea. Come back and tell me:

1. What did Jesus do?

2. How did his disciples (friends) feel as a result?

3. What does this teach us about Jesus?

CONSOLIDATION 1

Make a large boat out of boxes, chairs and tables and line it with a sheet or parachute. The boat must be big enough to contain all the children. One child is the mast and make a sail from a towel or second sheet. Once the

children are all in the boat tell the story with the children doing the sound effects. A leader can sprinkle water over the children when the storm gets up. Once the storm is under way the children can get out of the boat to be the waves, holding hands and running up to the boat, then retreating. When Jesus says, 'Be still!' the children stop still. Everyone gets into the boat for the wind-up.

WIND-UP 1

Remind the children of the warm-up and go over the answers to the questions. Can the children remember any other things that Jesus has authority over? Revise the memory verse, '*Jesus said, "I have been given all authority in heaven and on earth."' Matthew 28:18.*

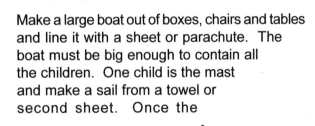

AUTHORITY OVER NATURE

Text: Mark 4:35-41

Teaching Point: Jesus has power over nature because he is God.

Memory verse: *Jesus said, "I have been given all authority in heaven and on earth." Matthew 28:18.*

WARM-UP 2

A leader enters dressed inappropriately for the current weather, e.g. in waterproofs carrying an umbrella on a sunny day, in shorts and T-shirt on a cold day, etc. The leader asks the children if he is dressed right for the weather? He explains that he is a weather forecaster. He puts up a simple map of the country and places the symbols appropriate to the current weather on the map (see visual aids for Lesson 21 Warm-up 2, page 50). He decides that he does not like that weather - he would prefer weather to go with what he is wearing. He is going to change the weather to suit him. He changes the weather symbols appropriately. Do the children believe he can do this? Come back at the end of the session and see if they are right.

Today's true story from the Bible is about the weather. Come back and tell me:

1. What did Jesus do?
2. How did his disciples (friends) feel as a result?
3. What does this teach us about Jesus?

CONSOLIDATION 2

Play a 'Shipwreck' type game. The children stand in the middle of the room with the leader facing them. Each time the leader calls out a command the children have to perform the appropriate action.

Demonstrate the actions to the children before the game starts. This game can be played as an elimination game if wished.

Command	Action
Wind	hands to mouth and blow.
Row to shore	move to the side of the room using a rowing action.
Raise the sail	pull down hands one after the other as though pulling on a rope.
Bale out	baling action as though emptying water.
Asleep	curl up on the floor with hands together by head.
Be still	freeze.
Rain	raise hands above head and bring them down with fingers waving.
Sun's out	lie flat on back as though sunbathing.

WIND-UP 2

Remind the children of the warm-up. Was the forecaster able to change the weather? Go over the answers to the warm-up questions. Why was Jesus able to control the weather? Because he is God. Revise the memory verse, '*Jesus said, "I have been given all authority in heaven and on earth."' Matthew 28:18.*

AUTHORITY OVER DEATH

Text: Mark 5:21-43

Teaching Point: Jesus has power over death because he is God.

Memory verse: *"I have been given all authority in heaven and on earth." Matthew 28:18.*

WARM-UP 1

Either, sit the children in a circle and talk about death, using pets, grandparents, etc. as examples. How did it make them feel? This works well with older children.

Or, bring in a dead plant. Ask the children to tell you how you can make it alive again. Try the different suggestions.

Today's true story is about someone who was dead. Come back and tell me:

1. Who was dead?

2. How did Jesus make her alive?

3. Why could Jesus do this?

CONSOLIDATION 1

For small children play a game to music. The children move around the room to music. When the leader shouts out, 'Dead!' and stops the music the children fall down on the ground. At the shout of 'Alive!' the music starts and the children get up and move around the room. This can be played as an elimination game if wished.

Or, divide the children into teams, each with a leader or older child as team captain. Give each team captain a set of 12 questions and answers from the Bible story. The team captain asks the first question. Once the correct answer is given one child runs to the end of the room, collects one word of the memory verse and returns to base. The second question is asked and the process repeated until all 12 words have been collected. The winner is the first team to collect their memory verse and put the words in the right order.

WIND-UP 1

Remind the children of the warm-up. Bring back the plant. Is it alive? Go over the answers to the warm-up questions. Why could Jesus bring the little girl back to life? Because he is God. Revise the memory verse.

AUTHORITY OVER DEATH

Text: Mark 5:21-43

Teaching Point: Jesus has power over death because he is God.

Memory verse: *"I have been given all authority in heaven and on earth."*   *Matthew 28:18.*

WARM-UP 2

Place a box on a table in clear view of the children. Bring out a selection of items one at a time, each time asking the children to identify whether that item is alive or dead. Place the live items on one table and the dead items on another one. Suggested items are a plant, twig, artificial flower, broom handle, piece of fruit, plastic toy fruit, soft toy animal, etc.

Today's true story is about someone who was dead. Come back and tell me:

1. Who was dead?

2. How did Jesus make her alive?

3. Why could Jesus do this?

CONSOLIDATION 2

Divide the children into teams. For each team prepare a set of pictures of Bible characters, each one named. Each set should contain 12 characters from the Bible story plus some random Bible characters, such as Samson, Mary, Ruth, David, Paul. (Use the basic man and woman shape found on page 52 and colour each

one differently.) Characters to use from the Bible story are Peter, James, John, Jairus, Jairus' wife, Jairus' daughter, sick woman, 2 messengers, 3 mourners. On the back of each of the pictures from the Bible story write one word of the memory verse. Write a random word on the back of each of the remaining pictures. Hide the Bible characters around the room. The teams look for their set of pictures, having been told the total number they must collect. Each team's set should be colour coded so that they only collect their own pictures. Having collected all the pictures the children must separate the story figures from the rest and place the story figures in the order in which they appear in the story. If they have it right they can turn over the pictures to give the memory verse.

WIND-UP 2

Remind the children of the warm-up. Which items are dead and which are alive? Go over the answers to the warm-up questions. Why could Jesus bring the little girl back to life? Because he is God. Revise the memory verse.

Lesson 4 Warm Up 1

Lesson 21 Warm Up 2

Lesson 4 Warm Up 1

Lesson 34 Warm Up 2

Lesson 21 Warm Up 2

AUTHORITY TO FEED

Text: Mark 6:30-44

Teaching Point: Jesus has power to provide for our needs because he is God.

WARM-UP 1

Prior to the session put up around the room a selection of different numbers on different coloured paper. Use one colour for 2-3 numbers. The numbers 2, 5 and 12 should all be on the same colour, whereas the remaining numbers must not be on that colour.

Tell the children there is a problem. On arrival you could only find 5 biscuits to give them with their drinks. Are there more than 5 children? How can we make it fair? The fairest thing is to share the biscuits out between all the children. Ask some leaders to help. Each leader takes 1 biscuit and breaks it into pieces, giving a piece to each child. Prime the leaders beforehand to ensure that there is not enough to go round. Search around and find 2 more biscuits to hand out. Make sure each child has had a bit, but some leaders have been left out. Ask if everyone has had a piece of biscuit. Did they have enough? Has any been left over?

Tell the children you have something to show them. Bring out 12 baskets. Count them out, showing that they are empty. What are they for?

Point to the numbers around the room. Ask the children to choose a number and a colour.

In today's true story from the Bible we will hear about 3 numbers. Tell the children to listen carefully so that they can tell you what those 3 numbers have to do with the Bible story.

CONSOLIDATION 1

Divide the children into teams. In the middle of the room place a collection of items, such as balls of newspaper, sponges, bottle tops, corks, drinking straws, plastic cups, etc. You need at least 20 of each item per team.

Stand the teams equidistant from the items. The leader calls out a number, either 2, 5 or 12. The first child from each team runs into the centre, picks up one item and returns to base. The second child runs into the centre, picks up one of the same items picked up by child 1 and returns to base. Children take it in turns to run until the number of the item collected equals the number called. A point is awarded to the first team to complete the task. The collected items are put to one side and must not be used again. The leader calls another of the three numbers and the game is repeated. As the number of items available for collection diminishes it is harder for team members to find the same item. At any point in the game an item being collected during that go can be returned to the centre and exchanged for a different one.

WIND-UP 1

Go over the answer to the warm-up question prior to the game. After the game remind the children of the warm-up and reinforce what the three numbers have to do with the Bible story. Why could Jesus do the miracle? Because he is God. Revise the memory verse using a rap. Clap hands twice, then clap thighs twice.

Clap	**clap**	**thigh**	**thigh**	
I	have	been	given	
all	auth	or	ity	
in	heaven	and	on	
earth.				*Repeat*
Matt	hew	twenty	eight	
verse	eight	een.		*Repeat*

54

AUTHORITY TO FEED

Text: Mark 6:30-44

Teaching Point: Jesus has power to provide for our needs because he is God.

WARM-UP 2

Two leaders are discussing how much food they will need for a party. First discuss how many guests are coming - could be 12, 20 or 50. How many sandwiches will be needed? How many cakes? How many jellies? Discuss how much is needed for each of the different number of guests. Ask the children to contribute the different foods needed and how much of each one is needed. List the items and amounts on a board. How much will be left over?

Today's true story from the Bible is about providing enough food for a large number of people. Come back and tell me:

   1. How many people needed feeding?

   2. How much food did they start with?

   3. How much was left over?

CONSOLIDATION 2

Divide the children into teams, each with an older child as captain, and tell them that they are waiters in a restaurant. A party of 8 people has booked, so they need to lay a table. Provide sheets of newspaper for tablecloths, serviettes, plastic cutlery and cups, paper plates, etc. Designate an area as the storeroom and place all the aforementioned items there. On the command to start each team must set up a table with the right amount of chairs and lay the table. Award points for quickness and appearance. Once the table has been laid for 8, tell the children that the party has increased to 16, so they must change the table to seat 16. Once the tables have been laid for 16, increase the number to 32. Make sure that there is not enough

items to lay the tables for 32. Finally reduce the number of the party to 6 so that the game ends with the children able to complete the task.

WIND-UP 2

Refer to the game and how difficult it was just laying a table for 32 people, especially as there was not enough stuff to go round. Remind the children of the warm-up and go over the answers to the questions. Point out that Jesus ended with more food than he started with. Is that what normally happens? We cannot do the impossible, such as laying a table for 32 people when there is not enough stuff to do so. Feeding 5,000 people with 5 loaves and 2 fish was impossible to do - but Jesus did it. Why could Jesus do it? Because he is God.

JESUS MADE A DEAF MAN HEAR

Text: Mark 7:31-37

Teaching Point: Jesus could make a deaf man hear because he is God.

WARM-UP 1

Set up the front area as a game show with a table and 2 chairs facing the children. Make a stand with 20 pieces of card or paper attached to 2 ring binders so that the pieces of card can be flipped back to show the piece underneath. Number each piece of card sequentially from 1-20, using one number per piece, with 20 on the top piece and 1 on the bottom. Place the stand on the table with the numbers in clear view of the children.

Leader 2 pretends to be deaf. Leader 1 introduces Leader 2 as someone who has something wrong with him. The children are allowed 20 questions to discover what is wrong. Questions can only be answered with 'yes' or 'no'. The 2 leaders sit at the table with the stand by Leader 1. Leader 1 answers the questions, each time flipping over a number so that the children can see how many questions they have left.

Once they have worked out what is wrong, ask the children how they can test it. Today's true story from the Bible is about someone who is deaf. Come back and tell me:

1. What else was wrong with the man?
2. How did Jesus make him better?

CONSOLIDATION 1

Play a listening game, such as Chinese Whispers. Sit the children and leaders in a circle. A leader whispers a phrase to the person on his or her left, who whispers that phrase to the person on their left, and so on around the circle until the phrase reaches the person on the right of the leader who started. The 2 phrases are compared to see how accurately the message has been passed. Do this 3 times, using the following phrases:

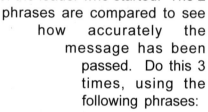

- Jesus took him off alone.
- Put his fingers in his ears.
- Ordered him not to tell anyone.

On the second round send the message around the circle in the opposite direction from the first round.

WIND-UP 1

Remind the children of the warm-up and go over the answers to the questions. Ask them to imagine how difficult life would be if they were deaf. There is so much that they would not understand. Refer to the game and point out how easy it was to misunderstand what was being said. God made our ears, therefore he can remake them. What does this story teach us about Jesus? He is God.

JESUS MADE A DEAF MAN HEAR

Text: Mark 7:31-37

Teaching Point: Jesus could make a deaf man hear because he is God.

WARM-UP 2

Skit or puppets (see script on page 78). Toby is jigging around to loud music. Trudy appears, very grumpy because she cannot concentrate on her homework with the music being so loud. She tells Toby to turn it off. Toby does not hear her. Trudy shouts louder and louder, but still Toby does not hear. Eventually Trudy asks the leader to turn the music off and he does so. Toby stops jigging and asks what is wrong. As Trudy tries to explain it becomes apparent that Toby cannot hear what she has been saying. He went to a disco the previous evening and the loud music has deafened him.

Today's true story from the Bible is about someone who is deaf. Come back and tell me:

1. What else was wrong with the man?
2. How did Jesus make him better?

CONSOLIDATION 2

The leader has a box containing a variety of objects that make a sound, such as a bell, cornflakes, squeaker, castanets, whistle, etc. Place pictures of all the items around the room so that they can be seen clearly by the children. The leader makes a sound with one of the objects, without the children seeing which object is used. The children listen carefully and run to the appropriate picture. Anyone going to the wrong picture misses a turn.

To make the game more difficult the leader can have a couple of items in the box that do not have corresponding pictures. In that case the children must be warned that they may hear a sound that does

not have a corresponding picture, in which case they stay where they are.

WIND-UP 2

Remind the children of the warm-up and go over the answers to the questions. Ask them to imagine how difficult life would be if they were deaf. There is so much that they would not understand. Refer to the game, reminding them how carefully they had to listen to get it right. How would they have managed if they were deaf? God made our ears, therefore he can remake them. What does this story teach us about Jesus? He is God.

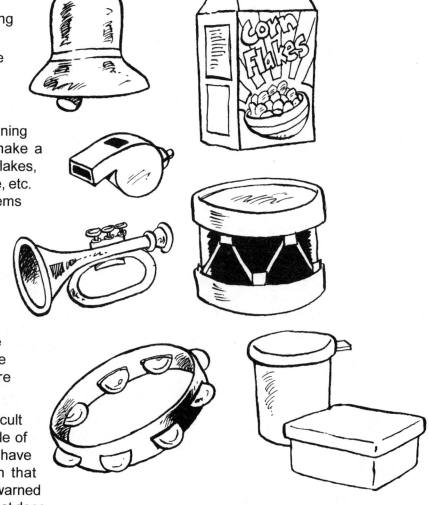

JESUS CALLS LITTLE CHILDREN

Text: Mark 10:13-16, Matthew 18:1-5

Teaching Point: Jesus' message is for children as well as adults.

Memory verse: *'Believe in the Lord Jesus and you will be saved.'* Acts 16:31.

WARM-UP 1

The leader asks for volunteers to perform specific tasks. The tasks must be suitable for children to perform. Any child volunteering is rejected, 'because he or she is only a child'. Each time an adult is selected to perform the task. Once all the tasks have been completed the leader says, 'Wasn't that nasty of me? Did you notice? I only chose adults. Couldn't children have done those jobs?'

Today's true story from the Bible is about children. Come back and tell me:

1. Who did not want the children to be there?
2. Who welcomed the children?

CONSOLIDATION 1

The children start at one end of the room with the leaders in the centre. The children have to run to the other end of the room (Jesus) without being tagged by a leader. Any child tagged is out. Repeat as wished.

If space is limited the leaders must stand still, but can reach down or to the side to tag children.

WIND-UP 1

Remind the children of the warm-up and how the leader did not want to use the children. Was Jesus like this? Who was? The disciples. Refer to the game and how the leaders tried to prevent the children reaching the other end (Jesus). That was like the disciples stopping children getting to Jesus. What did Jesus say to them? 'Do not stop children coming to me.' (Mark 10:14). Jesus wants children to be his friends.

WARM-UP 2

Place a box on a table in clear view of the children. Bring out a selection of items one by one, each time asking, 'Is this suitable for an adult or a child?' You could have some items suitable for both. Place the items in separate piles depending on whom they are for. Point out that different age groups need different things and can do different things.

Today's true story from the Bible is about children. Come back and tell me:

1. Who did not want the children to be there?
2. Who welcomed the children?

CONSOLIDATION 2

A crawling race. Divide the children into teams. For each team prepare a set of 12 pieces of paper with one word of the memory verse written on each. The teams start at one end of the room and the memory verse words are placed at the other end. Team members take it in turns to crawl down the room, pick up 1 memory verse word and crawl back. The second team member does not set off until the first one has returned. Once all the words have been collected the pieces of paper must be placed in memory verse order. The first team to complete the task wins.

Alternatively you could form 2 teams and play crawling football using a blown up balloon as a ball.

WIND-UP 2

Remind the children of the warm-up and go over the answers to the questions. Produce a leader dressed like a baby. When Jesus said that we have to become like little children did he mean that we have to be like this? Did he mean that we have to behave like a baby, like we did in the game, crawling everywhere? What did he mean? We must accept God's rule in our lives in the same way that a small child depends on his parents for his wellbeing.

JESUS MADE A BLIND MAN SEE

Text: Mark 10:46-52

Teaching Point: Jesus could make a blind man see because he is God.

WARM-UP 1

Seeing and believing. Prior to the lesson place a selection of articles in a large box. Place the box on a table in clear view of the children and ask them, 'Who believes that in this box there is a ......? Why?' Take out the articles one by one exactly as described. By the end why do they believe it? Because each time it has been true, as they have seen for themselves.

Today's true story from the Bible is about a man who saw because he believed and not the other way around. Come back and tell me:

1. How long had the man been blind?

2. How did Jesus heal him?

3. What did he learn about Jesus?

CONSOLIDATION 1

A blindfold game. Place the children in a circle with a blindfolded volunteer in the centre. Place a set of keys in the centre of the circle. The children take it in turns to creep round the circle and in to get the keys, without being heard by the blindfolded player. The player collecting the keys must return to the edge of the circle. If the blindfolded player can point to the player trying to get the keys the players swap places.

Alternatively, mark off an area and scatter various objects on the ground. Groups of children take it in turns to be blindfolded and find specified objects. This can be done as a team game with team members directing the blindfolded player.

WIND-UP 1

Remind the children of the warm-up and go over the answers to the questions. Ask them to think about how difficult life would be if they were blind. Refer to the game and how hard it was to do things when blindfolded. God made our eyes, therefore God can mend them. What did the blind man learn about Jesus? He is the promised Saviour. Jesus is God.

WARM-UP 2

Display a collection of items that can help with sight, such as binoculars, a sight card, a white stick, swimming goggles, spectacles, etc. Talk about each item and how they help.

Today's true story from the Bible is about a man who could not see. Come back and tell me:

1. How long had the man been blind?

2. How did Jesus heal him?

3. What did he learn about Jesus?

CONSOLIDATION 2

Form the children into pairs, one of which is blindfolded. Make an obstacle course using string markers and plastic cups or cushions. The blindfolded person must complete the obstacle course guided by the seeing partner. Once they reach the other end the children change places and repeat the exercise.

WIND-UP 2

Remind the children of the warm-up. Do any of those things help them to see Jesus? Go over the answers to the warm-up questions. Remind the children of the game and how they needed someone to guide them. Point out that, even when the blind man could see, he still needed Jesus to guide him. What did the blind man learn about Jesus? He is the promised Saviour. Jesus is God.

AT A WEDDING

Text: John 2:1-11

Teaching Point: As a result of Jesus demonstrating his glory his followers believed in him.

Memory verse: *Jesus is the Son of God. 1 John 4:15*

WARM-UP 1

Ask for a volunteer from the audience to help you. Place 2 stiff paper bags on the table and label one with the leader's name and one with the volunteer's name. (If you fold over the top of the bag twice the bag will stay open.) Between the bags place a row of 7 identical objects, such as oranges or apples. Tell the volunteer that you want to share the apples with him. Place one apple in each bag, starting with your own. Ask the volunteer to check that each bag contains one apple. Ask the children to watch carefully as you share out the remaining apples. Share out the remaining 5 one at a time in alternate bags, starting with **your** bag. (This will give 4 apples in your bag and 3 in the volunteer's bag.) Ask the children to tell you how many apples are in each bag. Agree that you have 4 apples and the volunteer only has 3. This is not fair. Remind the children that you had equal shares after depositing the first 2 apples in the bags. You need to take the last 5 apples out of the bags and start again. Take out 5 apples one at a time from alternate bags, starting with the **volunteer's** bag. (This will leave the volunteer with no apples and you with 2. The children will think that there is 1 apple in each bag.) Ask the children to watch carefully to make sure you get it right and share out the remaining 5 apples one at a time in alternate bags, starting with **your** bag. (This will give you 5 apples and the volunteer 2 apples.) Ask the children how many apples are in each bag? (They will think that you have 4 apples and the volunteer 3 apples.) This is still not right. Ponder on whether the problem is with the number of apples. Can you share out 7 apples equally between 2 people? Decide that you really only need 2 apples each, so you must replace 3 apples on the table. Take out 3 apples one at a time from alternate bags, starting with the **volunteer's** bag. (This will give you 4 apples and the volunteer none.) Ask the children how many apples are in each bag? (They will think that there are 2 apples in each bag.) Tell them that you have changed your mind and decided

to keep all 4 apples for yourself. When you say 'Abracadabra' the 2 apples in the volunteer's bag will change over into your bag. Say the word and ask the children if they believe the apples have changed over. Show them the volunteer's empty bag and ask the volunteer to take the 4 apples out of your bag and place them back on the table. Make sure that the children know this was only a trick.

In today's true story from the Bible Jesus really did change something. Come back and tell me:

1. What did he change?

2. What did this show about Jesus?

CONSOLIDATION 1

Divide the children into teams of no more than 7. Prepare a set of 7 memory verse words for each team, each set on a different coloured paper. Place each word in an envelope. Each team starts equidistant from a designated 'Exchange'. Give one set of memory verse words to each team and mark each team's home base with the colour of their memory verse. The object of the game is to be the first team to exchange their memory verse set for a different coloured set and place them in memory verse order.

On the command to start all team members run to the Exchange, change one word with a member from another team and return to base. They have a short period of time to look in their envelopes and decide which colour to collect. On command each team sends players with the words they want to exchange to repeat the process. Each player can only exchange one envelope. Continue until one team has completed the task. Teams can decide to change the colour they are collecting at any point in the game. If the game is going on too long call a halt and see which team has the most words of one colour. (The colour must be different from the one with which they started.)

AT A WEDDING

Text: John 2:1-11

Teaching Point: As a result of Jesus demonstrating his glory his followers believed in him.

Memory verse: *Jesus is the Son of God. 1 John 4:15*

WIND-UP 1

Remind the children of the warm-up. Did you really change the apples from one bag to another? No, it was just a magic trick. Jesus did not do magic tricks - he performed miracles. Go over the answers to the warm-up questions. Remind the children of the game and how they changed one colour for another. Once the task was completed, what did they learn about Jesus? Revise the memory verse.

WARM-UP 2

A skit or puppets (see script on page 79). A friend is getting married and has asked Toby and Trudy to organise the reception (wedding banquet). Toby and Trudy go through the list of items to make sure that they have not forgotten anything. They specify flowers, venue, food and drink. Toby ends his list with 50 jugs of water. Trudy asks what the water is for and is told it is to drink. Trudy is horrified - you do not drink water at a wedding!

Leader comments that it sounds as though that wedding reception might have a problem. Today's true story from the Bible is about a wedding reception where there was a problem. Come back and tell me:

1. What was the problem?

2. How was it solved?

3. What did this cause Jesus' disciples to do?

CONSOLIDATION 2

Divide the children into teams and provide each team with 2 hats and 2 scarves. Place one hat and scarf at the far end of the race course. The first player from each team dons a hat and scarf, runs to the far end, changes the hat and scarf for the one at that end and returns to base. Player 2 takes the hat and scarf from player 1, puts them on and repeats the process. Continue until all team

members have had a go. Alternatively, give each team member a white card, labelled 'water', to exchange for a red card, labelled 'wine'.

For a venue without space to run around, sit the children in a circle and hand each one a red or white card. The red cards are labelled 'wine' and the white cards 'water'. Pass the cards around to music. When the music stops those holding white cards are out. After each turn remove the same number of cards as children, making sure that some white cards remain each time. Continue until only 1 person is left.

WIND-UP 2

Remind the children of the warm-up and go over the answers to the questions. Remind the children of the game. They changed one hat and scarf for a different one (or a white card for a red one). This was an easy thing to do (and in the case of hat and scarf only temporary). When Jesus changed water into wine this was something no one else could do and it was a permanent change. What did this miracle cause Jesus' disciples to do? Put their faith in him (John 2:11).

A SICK SON

Text: John 4:46-54

Teaching Point: Jesus' miracles are designed to lead people to faith in him.

WARM-UP 1

Tell the children that you are a great magician. Do they believe you? You will show them how great you are by doing a very difficult trick. Ask for 2 volunteers and choose 2 of different sizes. Show them a rope and tie a knot in the middle incorporating a coloured handkerchief. Ask the children to check the knot. Is it really tight, etc? Stand the children at opposite ends of the front of the room and give each one an end of the rope to hold. Have some fun with them by pretending to pass the end of the rope to them and walking away before they have got hold of it. Once they have both ends of the rope, ask them to pull on the rope to check that the knot will not come undone. Place a teatowel (or similar) over the knot and handkerchief. Tell the children that when you say 'Abracadabra' and the 2 children pull on the rope the knot will come undone and the handkerchief fall to the ground. Say the magic word and the children pull on the rope. Nothing happens. Check under the teatowel to see that the knot and handkerchief are still there. Ask the children to help you by saying the magic word with you. Still nothing happens. Try a third time. Ask the children if you are really a great magician.

In today's true story from the Bible Jesus did something that really was amazing. Come back and tell me:

1. What did he do?

2. Who believed in Jesus as a result of the miracle?

3. How did they know that the healing had not happened by chance?

CONSOLIDATION 1

Divide the children into teams of roughly equal ability. Run a series of relay races, asking each time which team thinks that they will win. Suggested races are skipping, bunny hopping, running, flying like an aeroplane (running with arms outstretched at the sides), running backwards, etc. At the end of each race see whether the winning team was the one who said it would win.

WIND-UP 1

Talk about the game. Did people's actions match their words? Remind the children of the warm-up. Did your actions match your words? Go over the answers to the questions from the warm-up. What was it that caused the father to believe his son had not got better by chance? He started to get better at the very time Jesus had told the father his son would live (John 4:53). Remind the children about the warm-up. Remind them that the 'magic' you did was just a trick, but that what Jesus did was not magic or tricks it was real power, because he is the Son of God.

A SICK SON

Text: John 4:46-54

Teaching Point: Jesus' miracles are designed to lead people to faith in him.

WARM-UP 2

Ask for 2 volunteers and choose one child and one leader. Explain that the volunteers will take it in turns to be blindfolded and crawl down the room to a balloon which must be popped. Each one will have a seeing partner to direct them. Choose an older child to direct the child volunteer.

Line up the remaining children either side of the course. The child volunteer goes first. Ask the child if they trust the person to direct them along the right path. The child completes the task and bursts the balloon. (The child giving directions may need to be prompted by a leader.) Then the leader volunteer has a go. Let's see if he trusts me enough to do as I say. As each direction is given the blindfolded leader decides out loud whether or not he should obey it. Sometimes he does and sometimes he does not, depending on whether he thinks the direction sounds reasonable. He does not complete the task.

Today's true story from the Bible is about someone who wanted Jesus to do something for him and trusted him enough to do what he said. Come back and tell me:

1. Who was it?

2. What did he want Jesus to do?

3. What did he do in obedience to Jesus' command?

4. What 2 things happened as a result?

CONSOLIDATION 2

Divide the children into teams. Prepare a set of 9 cards for each team, each card contains one of the following letters: T R U S T O B E Y. The children start at one end of the room and each set of cards is randomly shuffled. 5 cards of the set are placed at the opposite end of the room and 4 at the start end. The leader calls out an action and on the command to start all the children race to the opposite end performing the designated action. The first team to get all its members to the other end scores a point. Each team picks up one card from the top of the pile. Repeat until all 9 cards have been collected. The first team to place the cards in order to spell 'TRUST' and 'OBEY' scores 2 points. Total up the points to see which team is the overall winner.

Suggested actions are running, skipping, bunny hopping, crawling, walking, jumping. Actions can be used more than once.

WIND-UP 2

Remind the children of the warm-up. Who demonstrated trust and how? The child volunteer by obeying the commands he was given. Go over the questions from the warm-up. The 2 things that happened as a result were the son being healed and the father and his household believing in Jesus (John 4:53). How did the father demonstrate that he believed in Jesus? By doing what he said. Remind the children of the game and how they demonstrated obedience by doing what the leader said. What words did they make in the game? 'Trust' and 'obey'. Trusting someone means believing what they say and acting on it. How do we show that we trust Jesus? By doing what he says. Where do we find this? In the Bible.

JESUS MADE A LAME MAN WALK

Text: John 5:1-15

Teaching Point: Jesus could make a lame man walk because he is God.

Memory verse: *Jesus is the Messiah, the Son of the living God. Matthew 16:16*

WARM-UP 1

Place a large box on a table in clear view of the children. One by one take out a selection of footwear and place them on the table. Ask the children to pair them up and state who would wear them when. E.g. a large pair of wellington boots would be worn by an adult in wet weather, a small pair of pink slippers with fur on would be worn by a girl indoors, a pair of rubber sandals would be worn on the beach, etc.

Today's true story from the Bible is about someone who did not need shoes. Come back and tell me:

1. Why did he not need shoes?
2. How long had he been like this?
3. What did Jesus do for him?

CONSOLIDATION 1

Divide the children into teams. Designate an area to be the pool and base the teams equidistant from it. Provide a mat at each team base. The team members take it in turns to race to the pool in the manner designated by the leader. A point is awarded for each individual race won. The children must move between mat and pool without using their feet, such as rolling, shuffling on bottom, squirming on front, dragged by 2 team mates on a mat. These can be used more than once. The winner is the team to accumulate the most points.

This game can be played as individuals when there are insufficient children to form teams.

WIND-UP 1

Remind the children of the warm-up and go over the answers to the questions. The man had no one to help him get to the pool. Think how difficult it must have been for him. Remind them of the game and how hard it was to get to the pool on their own. Why could Jesus make the lame man walk? Because he is God.

WARM-UP 2

Before the session prepare areas of the room as specific places, such as bedroom, library, shop, supermarket. Spread a sheet, parachute or similar on the floor at the front and sit on it. Explain that you cannot walk and you need help. Tell Leader 2 that you need to go to the library to get a book. Leader 2 offers to go for you. That's no good, because Leader 2 will not know which book to choose. Can't Leader 2 take you? Leader 2 cannot manage on his/her own. Ask for volunteers from the children to help. Ask the volunteers to drag you on the sheet to the library, where you choose a book. The volunteers drag you back to where you started. Do the same to the other venues - to choose some gloves at the shop, to decide which fruit you want at the supermarket. Finish by asking them to drag you to the bedroom to go to bed.

Comment on how hard it is not to be able to walk and having to be dragged around. Ask the volunteers if they found it hard. Would they want to do that all the time? Today's true story from the Bible is about someone who could not walk and had no one to help him. Come back and tell me:

1. How long had the man been lame?
2. What did he need help to do?
3. How did Jesus help him?

CONSOLIDATION 2

Divide the children into teams and give each team a bin liner full of soft items, representing the lame man, and a mat to drag it on. Prepare a set of memory verse words, one word per piece of paper, for each team. Place the shuffled memory verse words in a pile at the opposite end of the room from the team base. The children work in pairs, dragging the 'lame man' the length of the room, picking up a memory verse word and dragging the 'lame man' back again. The winner is the first team to collect their set of memory verse words and put them in the right order.

WIND-UP 2

Remind the children of the warm-up and game. How awful it was having to be dragged around everywhere, not just for the man but also for his friends. Go over the answers to the warm-up questions. How did Jesus make him better? By a word. Why could Jesus do this? Because he is God. Revise the memory verse.

A BLIND MAN

Text: John 9:1-41

Teaching Point: Spiritual healing is more important than physical healing.

WARM-UP 1

Display items that consist of something in a container, skin, case or shell, such as nuts, fruit, drink bottles, food packets, a wallet of coins. You also need the implements to open the containers and a bag for rubbish. Point out that the items are made of different parts, but one part is more important than the others. Pick an item and ask the children what is the most important part. Open it and, if appropriate, eat the contents. Do the same with other items.

Today's true story from the Bible is about something very important. Come back and tell me:

1. What was wrong with the man?
2. How did Jesus make him better?
3. What was the most important part of his healing?

CONSOLIDATION 1

Take 6 different packets of a type of food, such as cereal, lentils etc. Empty into plastic food bags and seal with sticky tape. Hide these plus other items, such as play money around the room. Also bag up some jigsaws. Divide the children into units of 3 or 4 and show them the empty containers. (If using play money you need some purses or wallets.) Tell the children to find the hidden items and match them with their containers. A point is scored for every matched item. Containers can hold more than one item, but the item must match, i.e. you cannot match cornflakes with a rice crispies box, even though both are cereals. Once all the items have been found and matched with their containers, add up the points scored to determine the winner.

WIND-UP 1

Ask the children what was the most important part of each item in the game - the container or the contents? Remind the children of the warm-up and go over the answers to the questions. What was the most important thing Jesus did for the blind man? He opened his spiritual eyes so that he could believe in Jesus.

WARM-UP 2

Find a picture of something that the children will have never seen, such as an animal or type of building. Pin up 4 large sheets of paper and ask for 4 volunteers. Give each one a pen and ask them to draw the thing, giving it its name. If the children do not recognise the name give them a brief general description, e.g. a tapir is an animal with 4 legs, (see page 51). The volunteers try and draw the animal. When they have finished compare their drawings with the true picture. How easy was it to draw something that they had never seen.

Today's true story from the Bible is about someone who could not see. Come back and tell me:

1. How long had he been blind?
2. How did Jesus heal him?
3. What was the most important part of his healing?

CONSOLIDATION 2

Divide the children into teams. At the opposite end of the room place a covered box with lots of different coloured items. Tell each team which colour to collect. The children take it in turns to run to the box, feel for an item and run with it back to base, regardless of its colour. After a few minutes stop the game. Count the number of correct items collected. Ask why they did badly? Could they have done better without the cover? Replace the items, remove the cover and replay the game. Increase the items to collect from 1 to 2 to 3 etc. Then bring the game to a close and count the coloured items collected. The team with the most correct items wins.

WIND-UP 2

Remind the children of the warm-up and go over the answers to the questions. Refer to the game and how difficult it was to collect the coloured items when they could not see them. Point out the importance of physical sight and how grateful the man was to be able to see. What was even more important than being able to see physically? To see that Jesus is the Saviour, the only one who can make us friends with God.

JESUS MADE A DEAD MAN LIVE

Text: John 11:1-44

Teaching Point: Jesus could make a dead man live because he is God.

Memory verse: *Jesus is the Messiah, the Son of the living God. Matthew 16:16*

WARM-UP 1

Ask the children, 'Who do you ask to help you when: you cannot reach a toy on a high shelf? you cannot do your sums? you need to cross a busy road?' For each scenario suggest who or what they might ask, such as other children, adults, animals, etc., including some which are ridiculous. Point out that, when you need help, you ask the person whom you know is able to help you.

Today's true story from the Bible is about 2 ladies who needed help. Come back and tell me:

1. What were their names?

2. Why did they need help?

3. Who did they ask for help?

4. How did that person help them?

CONSOLIDATION 1

Divide the group into multi-age teams of not more than 11 children, each team with a leader. Prepare a set of memory verse words per team. Write a word of the Bible verse and reference, onto each piece of card. Place the shuffled memory verse cards in piles at the opposite end of the room from the teams and give each team leader a set of 11 questions and answers from the passage. The questions should be age specific, so a younger child has an easier question than an older child. The leader reads out the questions one at a time. As each question is asked, the child who answers correctly runs to collect a word of the memory verse and brings it back to base. The winner is the first team to collect all 11 and put them in the correct order.

WIND-UP 1

Remind the children of the warm-up and go over the questions. Did Jesus give them the help they expected, i.e. heal Lazarus before he died? What Jesus did was even more amazing, he brought Lazarus back to life. Refer to the game. Why could Jesus bring Lazarus back to life? Because he is God. Revise the memory verse.

WARM-UP 2

Use a skit or puppets (see script on page 81). Trudy's pet (a soft toy) has died and she is sad. Toby asks her if she is sure it is dead? Is it breathing? Is it warm? Toby tries to give it something to eat. He listens to its heart. He pokes it to see if it will make a noise. Toby comments on how smelly it is. Trudy says it has been dead for a couple of days. Should she take it to the vet? Toby tells her that no-one can bring her pet back to life, it is well and truly dead.

Today's true story from the Bible is about someone who was dead. Come back and tell me:
1. Who was dead?

2. How do we know he was really dead?

3. How did Jesus heal him?

CONSOLIDATION 2

Play a game of tag. Choose a leader to be 'It' and one leader to be the rescuer. Any child tagged must fall to the ground or freeze. The rescuer moves around the room and rescues the children by saying child's name. Once rescued the child rejoins the game. Where space is a problem, this game can be played around a table. Designate one child as 'It'. All the other children place one hand on the table. 'It' attempts to touch one of the hands before it is snatched back from the table. No-one can move their hand until 'It' moves. If the hand is touched that child is out and places their head on the table. 'It' has another go. If 'It' misses the child missed becomes 'It'. Children who are out are brought back in by the leader touching them and saying child's name.

WIND-UP 2

Remind the children of the warm-up and go over the answers to the questions. Refer to the game. How were the 'dead' children brought back to life? How did Jesus bring Lazarus back to life? Why could Jesus do this? Because he is God.

THE SERVANT KING

Text: John 13:1-38

Teaching Point: Our love for God and for one another is demonstrated by our service.

WARM-UP 1

Prepare 4-5 small paper plates, on each of which is written a combination of different foods and quantities for a party. E.g. 5 crisps, 1 chocolate biscuit, 2 fizzy drinks; 10 crisps, 3 chocolate biscuits, water. Include some that are less appealing, such as 1 prune wrapped in bacon, 2 plain crackers, 1 soda water. Ask 4-5 volunteers to come out and each choose a plate. Ask the volunteers to read out what is on their plate, then give each volunteer the opportunity to swap their plate for someone else's. Discuss why they made a swap and what happened to the most appealing plate. The likelihood is that each child will have wanted that plate for him/herself.

Today's true story from the Bible is about someone who did not seek the best for himself. Come back and tell me:

1. Who was it?
2. What did he do?
3. Why did he do it?

CONSOLIDATION 1

The aim of the consolidation is to highlight the characteristics of a servant. Divide the group into teams of 6-10 children. For each team prepare a set of words that describe a servant (see below) and write one letter on each piece of card. The cards should be colour-coded, with each team having a different colour. Hide the cards around the room. The teams hunt for their colour cards and piece them together to make their words. Points are awarded for each correct word and extra points are given if the team can give the meaning of the word. Teams need not have the same words to put together. (For younger children cut out the cards in a zigzag pattern to make it easier to fit the letters together to form words.)

Suggested words: humble, loyal, truthful, obedient, polite, honest, hardworking.

WIND-UP 1

Talk about the words made in the consolidation and how they apply to a servant. Remind the children of the warm-up. Would a servant want the best plate for himself or would he want it for his master? Go over the answers to the warm-up questions. How did Jesus serve his disciples? How can we show our love for Jesus by serving each other?

WARM-UP 2

On a flipchart or similar draw up a time chart covering a day and evening with times down the left-hand side. Divide the chart into 2 columns, heading the left one 'Master' and the right one 'Servant'. In the left-hand column record the various activities of the master, e.g. getting dressed, breakfast, working at his desk, lunch with guests, meeting people, horseriding, dinner with guests, preparing for bed. Ask the children to volunteer what the servant does to help his master and fill in the chart.

Discuss whom the servant puts first and how. Today's true story from the Bible is about Jesus. Come back and tell me:

1. Who is Jesus putting first in the story?
2. Why?
3. How should we follow his example?

CONSOLIDATION 2

Form the children into 1 or more circles, with the children standing at arm's length from each other. Ask for 2 volunteers, one to be the farmer and one the fox. The fox has a 3-second start on the farmer and sets off weaving in and out through the children. The farmer must follow the same pattern as he tries to catch the fox. Change the volunteers every 2-3 minutes, until everyone who wants to has had a turn.

WIND-UP 2

Remind the children of the warm-up and go over the answers to the questions. Ask all the children who were caught in the game to stand up. Point out that they lost their lives in the game. What was the biggest thing that Jesus did for us? He laid down his life for us, so that we can live forever with God. Discuss how we show our love for Jesus by serving one another.

THE REJECTED KING

Text: John 18:28 - 19:42

Teaching Point: Jesus' death on the cross was according to God's plan.

WARM-UP 1

Place on a table a selection of items suitable for building a tower. Choose 3-6 people to build the tallest tower they can from these items, either individually or in pairs. They are allowed to change their design as often as they wish, even if this is to copy someone else.

When they have finished discuss how well the towers were built and whether or not plans were changed. Today's true story from the Bible is about a very special plan. Come back and tell me:

1. Who made the plan?
2. What did the plan achieve?

CONSOLIDATION 1

Divide the children into teams and give each team a selection of equipment, such as boxes, mats, newspaper, etc. Give each team a different item to design and build, using the equipment provided. When they have finished judge the results.

WIND-UP 1

Review the various items designed in the game. Did their initial plan work or did they need to change it? Remind the children of the warm-up and point out any plans that needed changing and why. Go over the answers to the warm-up questions. Point out that God only ever had one plan to rescue people and make it possible to have their sins forgiven. Jesus was the perfect sacrifice, who would die to pay the penalty for our wrong-doing. This was always the perfect and only plan.

WARM-UP 2

Divide the children into teams. Ask them to form various modes of transport, such as car, train, aeroplane, using only their bodies. When they have finished judge the results. Discuss how they set about the exercise - did they have a plan before they started forming the item, was the plan changed during the process and why?

Today's true story from the Bible is about a very special plan. Come back and tell me:

1. Who made the plan?
2. What did the plan achieve?

CONSOLIDATION 2

Divide the children into teams and place a large number of items in a pile in the centre. Appoint home bases for each team that are equidistant from the centre. The object of the game is to see if the teams take items from the central store that match with those on the leader's list. E.g. the leader calls out 6 items, having on his list 3 disposable cups and 3 pencils. The teams must decide which combination of items to collect and bring back to base. No team member can collect items from the centre until the leader calls out, 'Good Friday!'. After each turn display your list and see if there are any winners. Only give a team a point if they get all the items on your list correct, i.e. their plan agrees perfectly with your plan. All items are returned to the centre after each turn.

WIND-UP 2

Remind the children of the warm-up and go over the answers to the questions. Point out that we are always changing our plans as circumstances change. God's plan for salvation was always that Jesus would pay the penalty for our sins by dying on the cross. There was never any other plan.

THE RISEN KING

Text: John 20:1-29

Teaching Point: Jesus' resurrection is our only source of hope.

Memory verse: *Trust in the Lord with all your heart. Proverbs 3:5*

WARM-UP 1

Prepare several containers with what is written on the outside differing from the container's contents, e.g. a biscuit tin with bread, a cake tin with cheese. All the containers should contain something unexpected, such as food containers with a bag of nails. Hold up the containers one by one and ask the children to guess what is inside. Display the contents to see if they were right. At the end ask the children what the contents had in common - they were totally unexpected.

In today's true story from the Bible something unexpected happened. Come back and tell me:

1. What happened?
2. How did the disciples react?

CONSOLIDATION 1

Seeing is believing. Divide the group into teams of 6. Two teams play at a time. One member of each team is blindfolded and the others stand in a line facing each other. The blindfolded members take turns to pick the opposing team in order of height, picking the tallest child first, then the next tallest, and so on. In order to get a clue, the blindfolded child is allowed to touch a member of the opposite team, who must recite the memory verse. The picked children line up in the order picked. At the end remove the blindfolds and award points. Each child in the line up is worth points. When choosing from a line up of 6 children, if the tallest child is chosen award 6 points, if the second tallest is chosen award 5 points, and so on down to 1 point for the shortest child chosen. When choosing from a line up of 5 children, start with 5 points for the tallest and 4 points for the tallest when choosing from a line up of 4 children. The other teams can either do the same or could choose the shortest child.

WIND-UP 1

Remind the children of the warm-up and go over the answers to the questions. Were the disciples expecting Jesus to rise from the dead? Comment on how overjoyed they were. Refer to the game and how difficult it was to choose the right child when you could not see. Some disciples found it difficult to believe that Jesus had come back to life until they actually saw him.

WARM-UP 2

Prepare several challenges with promises attached, e.g. if you do 10 star jumps I will give you a sweet. Ask for volunteers. Keep your promise for the majority, but fail to keep it for a few. Then ask the children how they felt when you kept your promise and when you didn't.

In today's true story from the Bible we learn about a very special promise. Come back and tell me:

1. What was the promise?
2. Was it kept?
3. How did the disciples react?

CONSOLIDATION 2

For children over 6 years the following activity is achievable. Divide into teams of 8 and give each child an empty milk bottle. Give each team a jug of water and a funnel. The children fill the bottles to different heights so that each bottle makes a different note when tapped with a spoon. This is done by trial and error. Each team needs an adult to supervise. Once they have finished filling their bottles they practise a simple tune. Ask the teams to play their tunes to each other. This is **not** a competitive game.

Younger children can move around the room to music. When the music stops they fall down 'dead'. When the leader shouts, 'Jesus is alive!' the children jump up and the music restarts.

WIND-UP 2

Remind the children of the warm-up and go over the questions. Comment on how overjoyed the disciples were at Jesus' resurrection. He had come back to life, just as he had promised. Jesus was no longer dead, but alive and the disciples job was to tell others about it.

THE FORGIVING KING

Text: John 21:1-19

Teaching Point: God is willing to use anyone who truly repents.

WARM-UP 1

The warm-up is designed to teach the meaning of forgiveness. Ask for volunteers to take it in turns to scribble on a flip chart. Once the paper is covered with scribble, tear it off, screw it into a ball and throw it away. Ask for volunteers to make a mess on a table or the floor by scattering stale cereal or pulses. Sweep them up and throw them away. Point out that this is what happens to our sins when Jesus forgives us. It is as though the sin had never happened.

Today's true story from the Bible is about someone who was forgiven. Come back and tell me:

1. Who was he?
2. What had he done?
3. How do we know he was forgiven?

CONSOLIDATION 1

Divide into mixed-age teams, ensuring that each team contains some small children. The 2 strongest team members start at their base and the remaining members start at the opposite end of the room. The 2 strong members must run to the other end of the room, pick up a team member and return to base. This continues until all the team members have been transported to their home base. Before the game starts the children must be shown how to transport others safely by interlocking their hands, left to left and right to right, to make a seat. This game can also be played using a plastic sledge or washing basket to transport the children.

WIND-UP 1

Remind the children of the warm-up and go over the questions. Comment on Peter denying Jesus. How do we know he was forgiven? Jesus gave him a job to do. He had to look after Jesus' sheep (other Christians). Remind the children of the game and how the strongest had to transport the others back to their home base. Once we have been forgiven (reconciled with God) we, too, must care for others.

WARM-UP 2

Use a skit or puppets to demonstrate that saying sorry has to be accompanied by true repentance (see script on page 82). Toby tells Trudy that he has got a ticket for tonight's football game. Trudy points out that the last time Toby wanted to go to a football match Dad refused to let him go in case he got hurt. Toby says he is not going to ask Dad, but will just go. When he returns Trudy tells him that Dad is very angry and wants to see Toby straight away. Toby says not to worry, he will go and say he is sorry, then Dad will not punish him. Trudy asks if he is really sorry. Toby says, no; he is going to another match next week.

The leader asks the children whether Dad should forgive Toby if he is not really sorry? Today's true story from the Bible is about someone who was truly sorry for what he had done. Come back and tell me:

1. Who was he?
2. What had he done?
3. How do we know he was forgiven?

CONSOLIDATION 2

Run a limbo dancing competition. Two leaders hold a pole and the children pass under it one at a time to music, without allowing any part of their body to touch the ground apart from their feet. Lower the pole each round until there is a winner, who gets a small prize.

WIND-UP 2

Remind the children of the warm-up and go over the answer to the questions. Talk about the game. Point out that each child was disqualified as they failed to get under the bar. We would all be disqualified from going to heaven if it depended on our own efforts, but Jesus is a forgiving king, whose forgiveness enables us to go to heaven when we die. Jesus has promised that he will forgive everyone who is truly sorry and asks him to save them (1 John 1:9).

Lesson 39

THE LORDS PRAYER

Enter Toby humming, carrying a tube of Smarties.

Leader: Hello, Toby. You're looking very pleased with yourself.

Toby: (*surprised*) Oh! Hi [Leader's name]. I didn't see you there.

Leader: Aren't you going to say hello to the others?

Toby: I suppose so. Hello, boys and girls.

   (Wait for response from audience.)

Toby: That wasn't very loud. Try again. After me: Hello, boys and girls.

   Wait for response from audience.

Toby: That's better. (*Starts to exit.*)

Leader: Wait a bit. Where are you going?

Toby: Somewhere. I really do need to go.

Leader: What are you carrying, Toby?

Toby: (*looks at empty hand*) Umm, nothing.

Leader: In your other hand, silly.

Toby: Ah, that. A tube of Smarties.

Leader: Where did you get them?

Toby: (*thinks*) I borrowed them.

Leader: What do you mean, you borrowed them? Are you going to give them back?

Toby: Yeees.

Leader: How many do you have left?

Toby: [*Shaking tube vigorously*] None!

Leader: How can you give them back when you've already eaten them? Who did you borrow them from?

Toby: [*Looking around slowly*] Weeellll, they were on a table at your place.

Leader: My place! They were mine. You didn't ask me for them!

Toby: [*Hangs head in shame*] I asked Jughead.

Leader: Who's Jughead?

Toby: Jughead is the little voice I hear that always tells me it is right to do naughty things.

Leader: Why do you listen to someone who tells you to do the wrong thing?

Toby: Because I don't know who else to talk to.

Leader: [*Turns to audience*] In today's true story from the Bible we will learn whom we should talk to whenever we have a problem.

THE THREE SERVANTS

The leader explains that he has been visiting some friends. They have 2 children, Toby and Trudy. He is just about to leave and needs to call Toby and Trudy to say goodbye.

Leader: Toby, Trudy, can you come here a minute?

(Pause)

Leader: Those two are never around when you want them. I wonder where they are? Have you seen them? *(Pause)* I wonder if they're hiding. Perhaps they didn't hear me. Will you help me call them? All together now, 1 2 3 Toby! Trudy! Where are you?

(Pause)

Leader: They're still not here! If they don't come soon, I'll have to go without saying goodbye.

(While the Leader is talking, Toby and Trudy take turns to peer over the screen, then disappear again. Hopefully children will call out when they appear, but the Leader cannot see them. Eventually:)

Leader: What a shame. I shall have to go without saying goodbye, and I don't know when I'll be back. I wanted to give them a present before I go ….

(Toby and Trudy shoot up into view.)

Toby: Did you say a present?

Trudy: Ssh! Oh, Uncle [Leader's name], is it time for you to go already? Doesn't time fly? We **will** miss you.

Toby: Yes, we **will** miss you. Even if it is years.

Leader: I shall miss you two as well. I just wanted to say goodbye and to give you a little present.

Toby: A present for me? Yes please.

Trudy: It's very kind of you to give **us** something, Uncle [Leader's name].

Toby: What are you going to give us?

Leader: Here's £10 for each of you. *(Counts out 2 piles of 10 £1 coins onto the table.)* Now, this is a lot of money and you're to spend it wisely. You're not to waste it.

Trudy: We won't waste it, Uncle […]. We'll spend it really, really carefully, won't we Toby?

Toby: Yes, I'll be very careful how I spend mine, Uncle […].

Trudy: So will I!

Leader: Well, it's time for me to go, so goodbye. I'll come and see you again when I can. Be good, and remember, spend that money wisely!

(Leader disappears to one side.)

Trudy: What are you going to spend your money on, Toby?

Toby: I don't know. I'll have to really think about it. Uncle […] said we have to spend it carefully.

Trudy: I'm going to spend all mine on sweets. I can have chocolates, and fruit gums, and lollipops, and bubble gum, and gobstoppers, and sherbert, and licorice, and Turkish delight, and ….

Toby: A big stomach ache! I like sweets too. Can we share them?

Trudy: No! you've got your own money! If you want sweets buy them yourself!

Toby: OK I will! But I'm going to save £5 for holidays, and £2 to buy Christmas presents, and £2 for birthday presents. That will leave me *(pause)* £1 for sweets.

Trudy: What a dope. What's the point of saving it when you can spend it on things you want?

Toby: When Uncle […] said we must spend it wisely, do you think he meant us to spend it all on ourselves?

Trudy: I don't know. I don't really care. After all, it's not as though he's ever going to find out, is it?

Toby: He might ask us next time he comes what we've spent it on.

Trudy: No he won't. Grown-ups always say things they don't really mean. They usually forget. That is what growing old is all about - losing your memory and your money!

Toby: Dad didn't forget when he told me if I broke another window with my football I'd have to pay for it.

Trudy: That's different. Uncle […] will forget. After all, he's over 30 and he may not come back at all. Mm, just look at all that money. Doesn't it look good? It feels so good just to know I've got it there. Perhaps I won't spend it after all - at least, not just yet.

(Enter Matilda, carrying a sponsorship form.)

Toby: Hello Matilda. Out on day release are we?

Matilda: Oh, Toby and Trudy, am I glad to see you two.

Toby: Why?

Matilda: My school is rebuilding the science lab that burnt down and we all have to help.

Toby: How?

Matilda: We're asking our friends to sponsor us. I've promised to run round the playground as many times as I can without stopping and I have to get 10 people to sponsor me. Look, I've already got 8, and if you two will do it I'll have the 10 I need.

Toby: How much do we have to pay?

Matilda: Most people have promised to pay 10p a lap and the most I can do is 10 laps.

Trudy: *(horrified)* That's £1 if you do 10 laps!

Toby: Well, Uncle […] has just given us £10 each, and it is for a good cause.

Trudy: So? It's not my school, so why should I care?

Toby: Matilda is your best friend. She needs 2 more sponsors. We could help her.

Trudy: But if I give Matilda's silly old school £1 I'll only have £9 to spend on sweets.

Toby: You're so selfish, Trudy. Come on, Matilda, I'll sign your form for you.

Matilda: Thank you Toby. You're a real friend.

Trudy: I thought you were going to save £9 Toby. Now you'll only have £8 left!

Toby: No. I still need the £9 for holidays and presents, so shall give the other pound to Matilda and go without the sweets.

(Toby and Matilda exit.)

Trudy: You're stupid, Toby. You'll be sorry. Ooh, doesn't that money look good. Let's think of all the different sweets I can buy. Chocolate. *(Pause)* And fruit gums. *(Pause)* And lollipops. And bubblegum. And gobstoppers. And sherbert. And licorice. And Turkish delight. Mm.

(Trudy disappears.)

Leader: Which one did the right thing with the money I gave them? Toby or Trudy? Today's true story from the Bible is a story Jesus told to his friends. I want you to come back and tell me what the people were given and what they did with it.

THE CRUCIFIXION

A packet of foil wrapped chocolate Easter eggs (or similar) is on the table. It is empty apart from the foil wrappings. Toby enters and looks around..

Toby: Hello, boys and girls. Are you looking forward to Easter? I am. Do you like Easter eggs? I do. I think they are just scrummy. (*looks around*) Have you seen Trudy? Will you help me call her? Trudy! Trudy! Where are you?

(*Wait for response from audience.*)

Toby: That wasn't loud enough. Trudy won't hear you unless you really shout. Try again. On the count of 3. 1 2 3 Trudy! Trudy! Where are you?

(*Trudy pops into view.*)

Trudy: What's all that noise? How can I sleep with all that racket going on?

Toby: Sleep? Do you know what time it is? It's [current time]. You should have been up ages ago.

Trudy: Why? What's so special about today?

Toby: It's nearly Easter. And I really enjoy Easter.

Trudy: So do I. All the lovely things to eat, like hot cross buns and Easter eggs.

Toby: Ummm.

Trudy: (*spots the packet of Easter eggs*) Hey, Toby! Have you seen that packet of Easter eggs?

Toby: Where? Oh, those. Yes, they're mine. Would you like one?

Trudy: Yes please. (*to leader 2*) Can you hand me one please?

(*Leader looks in the packet to find it full of foil wrappings and no eggs.*)

Leader 2: Looks like they've all been eaten. There's only foil wrappers here.

Trudy: Have you eaten them all, Toby?

Toby: Um, looks like it. They were very nice.

Trudy: You are greedy, Toby. There's nothing left for me.

Toby: You can always have some of the foil wrappings to make something.

Trudy: I suppose so.

(*Leader 2 puts some of the foil wrappings in front of Trudy. Enter Leader 1.*)

Leader 1: (*to children*) I've brought in a packet of Easter eggs to give you all one and I can't find it anywhere. Have any of you seen it?

(*Waits for response from children. Leader 1 looks in the wrong place, but eventually follows the children's directions and spots the packet of eggs. Meanwhile puppets disappear.*)

Leader 1: Ah, there they are.

(*Leader 1 picks up the packet to find it is empty.*)

Leader 1: They're all gone. I know who's eaten them - Toby and Trudy. (*looks round to find they have gone.*) Toby! Trudy! Come back here this minute.

(*Puppets slowly reappear in previous place so that foil wrappings are in front of Trudy.*)

Leader 1: (*shaking the empty packet*) Which of you has eaten these chocolate eggs? Was it you, Toby?

Toby: No, it wasn't me.

Trudy:	Toby, you liar!
Leader 1:	Are you sure it wasn't you, Toby?
Toby:	How can it have been me? It's Trudy who has the foil wrappers.
Trudy:	But, but, but…
Leader 1:	Not another word, Trudy. I am really disappointed in you. I thought you knew better.
Trudy:	But I…
Leader 1:	I don't want to hear any excuses. Go to your room. (*To Toby*) You go and get ready, Toby, and we will go to the circus (or similar).

(Toby leaves humming cheerfully.)

Leader 2:	(*to children*) Did Trudy eat the chocolate eggs? Should she have been punished? In today's true story from the Bible somebody else gets a punishment they don't deserve.

AUTHORITY OVER NATURE

The leader introduces 2 friends who have come to visit this morning, Toby and Trudy.

Trudy appears.

Trudy: Hello, boys and girls. *(Looks round.)* Have you seen my brother, Toby? Wherever we go he's always late. *(Calls)* Toby. Toby.

    (Pause while nothing happens.)

Trudy: Perhaps if you all give him a call he'll come. All together now, Toby, Toby. That wasn't loud enough. Try again. On the count of 3 call out, Toby, where are you? 1, 2, 3 Toby, where are you?

(Enter Toby.)

Toby: What's all that noise for? Anybody would think I'm deaf!

    Hello, Trudy. Who are all those boys and girls?

Trudy: It's the Sunday School, Toby. Don't you remember? [Leader's name] asked us if we'd like to come to Sunday School with him.

Toby: Oh, that's right. I do remember now. What do you do at Sunday School, Trudy?

Trudy: [Leader's name] said they sing songs, then have a story, then play a game.

Toby: I'm not that keen on singing, Trudy.

Trudy: I think we've missed that bit.

Toby: That's all right then. I like stories. Do you think we've missed that? Have we missed the story, boys and girls?

(Response)

Trudy: Oh good, 'cos I like stories too. I 'specially like stories where everyone lives happily ever after.

Toby: Huh, girls! I heard a really good story at school this week, Trudy.

Trudy: What was it about?

Toby: It was all about a king who lived hundreds of years ago.

Trudy: Was he real?

Toby: I think so. He was a Viking.

Trudy: What's a Viking?

Toby: They came from a country up north somewhere, I think. Its called Scan something.

Trudy: Do you mean Scotland?

Toby: No, it's further away than that. Oh I remember, it's called Scandinavia. They came in big boats and fought against the people of England.

Trudy: Who won?

Toby: The Vikings, silly. Otherwise he couldn't have been king, could he?

Trudy: Oh I suppose not. Well what was the king called?

Toby: King Canute.

Trudy: I've never heard of him. What did he do?

Toby: Well, he thought he was so powerful that he could do anything. He thought he could even tell the sea what to do!

Trudy:	He never!
Toby:	He did!
Trudy:	He must have been mad. **No-one** can tell the sea what to do.
Toby:	Well he did. He went down to the beach, and he stood there, and he waited for the tide to start coming in.
Trudy:	What happened next?
Toby:	Well, the tide started to come in, and King Canute told the tide to stop.
Trudy:	He didn't?
Toby:	He did.
Trudy:	Well, what happened? Did the tide stop?
Toby:	What do you think?
Trudy:	I think that if the tide had stopped everyone would know about it, don't you?
Toby:	Had you ever heard about King Canute before today?
Trudy:	No.
Toby:	Well, then. Do you think the tide did as it was told?
Trudy:	Of course not.
Toby:	You're right, it didn't.
Trudy	I bet he looked silly.
Toby:	I bet he got wet. After all, no-one can tell the sea what to do, can they, Trudy?
Trudy:	You're right, Toby. No-one can tell the sea what to do.

(Puppets remain visible until the children have gone.)

JESUS MADE A DEAF MAN HEAR

Toby appears, jigging around to loud music. Trudy shoots into view, very angry.

Trudy: (*shouts*) Toby! How can I do my homework while you are making that awful noise? Turn it off!

(Pause while nothing happens.)

Trudy: Toby! Did you hear me? I said, Turn that music off before it sends me stark, staring mad!

(Pause while nothing happens.)

Trudy: Toby! Urghhhhh. Will you help me, boys and girls? Perhaps if we all shout as loud as we can he will hear us? All together now, on the count of 3,   1   2   3   Toby! Toby!

(Pause while nothing happens.)

Trudy: (*to leader*) [Leader's name], please can you turn off the music?

(Leader turns off the music.)

Toby: (*stops jigging*) Hey? What did you do that for?

Trudy: For me! I cannot hear myself think when you play your music as loud as that.

Toby: Eh? What did you say?

Trudy: (*louder*) I said, I cannot hear myself think when you play your music that loud.

Toby: You really must speak up, Trudy. I can't hear a word when you whisper like that.

Trudy: (*shouting*) I'm not whispering. I'm **shouting**. What's wrong with you?

Toby: Nothing. I just can't hear you very well. (*To audience*) And that's a good thing!

Trudy: (*loudly*) What did you say?

Toby: Nothing.

Trudy: (*loudly*) Hm! So why can't you hear properly?

Toby: I don't know. I didn't realise I couldn't until you shouted at me.

Trudy: (*loudly*) Were you alright yesterday?

Toby: I think so.

Trudy: (*loudly*) So what did you do yesterday?

Toby: Oh, Trudy, I had a great time. I went to a disco with my friends. The music was fantastic! That's why I've been playing it today.

Trudy: (*loudly*) But, Toby, the music's made you deaf. You really **must** turn it down or you'll never get your hearing back.

Toby: What did you say? Honestly, Trudy, you must learn to speak up.

(Toby exits jigging and singing to himself.)

Trudy: (*loudly*) Toby! Just listen to me.

(Trudy exits.)

AT A WEDDING

Trudy appears and looks around

Trudy: Hello, boys and girls. Have you seen Toby? I must find him. My friend, Jemima, is getting married and she's asked us to organise her wedding reception. I'm so excited. (*calls*) Toby! Toby!

(Pause while nothing happens.)

Trudy: Oh, I wonder where he is? Can you help me call him? We'll say, Toby! Toby! Where are you? Are you ready? All together on the count of 3, 1 2 3 Toby! Toby! Where are you?

(Pause while nothing happens.)

Trudy: That obviously wasn't loud enough. Let's make it really loud this time. All together now, on the count of 3, 1 2 3 Toby! Toby! Where are you?

(Toby enters.)

Toby: Hey, there's no need to shout. I heard you the first time.

Trudy: Well why didn't you come?

Toby: I was busy. Anyway, now I'm here I may as well **hear** what it is you want.

Trudy: Jemima's getting married.

Toby: Never. Who would want to marry her?

Trudy: Honestly, Toby. You are mean. Jemima's lovely. Anyway, she's getting married and guess what?

Toby: What?

Trudy: She's asked us to organise her wedding reception.

Toby: You're joking, aren't you?

Trudy: No.

Toby: How can we organise a wedding reception? We wouldn't know what to do.

Trudy: Don't worry, it won't be difficult. We just need to make a list. [Leader's name] will help us.

Toby: OK. What should we put on the list?

Trudy: Well, we definitely need flowers.

(Leader lists things as they are mentioned.)

Toby: Why do we need flowers?

Trudy: You've got to have flowers. They make the room look pretty.

Toby: OK. So we need flowers. What else?

Trudy: We need a room to hold it in.

Toby: Yeh, we'd look pretty silly with nowhere to meet.

Trudy: And we need tables.

Toby: And chairs!

Trudy: And tablecloths. I told you this would be easy.

Toby: So that's flowers, and a room and tables and chairs and tablecloths. What else?

Trudy: Food!

Toby: Ooh yes! We must have food. What sort? (*to the children*) Can you help us?

(*Leader lists children's suggestions. Puppets ask children for clarification regarding quantities.*)

Toby: And 50 jugs of water.

Trudy: Did you say, 50 jugs of water?

Toby: Yes. You have to have plenty to drink at weddings.

Trudy: Toby! People don't drink water at weddings!

Toby: Yes they do. I read it somewhere.

Trudy: Oh well, if you're sure. It doesn't sound right to me.

(*Puppets exit.*)

JESUS MADE A DEAD MAN LIVE

Trudy appears, sobbing quietly. There is an rabbit (soft toy) lying on the table. Toby enters, humming to himself, stopping abruptly when he sees Trudy.

Toby: Hey, Trudy, you're crying. What's the matter?

Trudy: My pet rabbit's died.

Toby: What, Peter?

Trudy: Yes. (*Trudy snuffles.*) He's over there.

Toby: Are you sure he's dead, Trudy?

Trudy: I think so. He's not moving.

Toby: He might just be asleep. Hadn't we better check he's not breathing?

(Puppets watch carefully.)

Toby: He doesn't appear to be breathing.

Trudy: I told you he's dead. I'm so unhappy.

Toby: Perhaps if we give him something to eat he'll get better. Rabbits really like lettuce.

(Leader offers the rabbit a lettuce leaf, but nothing happens.)

Trudy: I told you he was dead. I'm so sad.

Toby: Just wait a minute, Trudy. Perhaps he's just not hungry. We haven't listened to his heart yet.

(Leader listens to the rabbit's heart and shakes his head sadly.)

Trudy: He's dead, Toby. I told you so.

Toby: He feels a bit cold. Perhaps he just needs warming up.

(Leader puts a blanket around the rabbit. Puppets wait to see if anything happens.)

Toby: We could try poking him to see if he makes a noise.

(Leader pokes the rabbit.)

Trudy: Toby, I told you he's dead. Just leave him alone.

Toby: Perhaps he just needs the kiss of life, Trudy. (*Moves towards the rabbit*) Oh, he does smell a bit. How long has he been like this for?

Trudy: A couple of days.

Toby: Well, if he's been like this for a couple of days of course he's dead.

Trudy: Do you think I should take him to the vet?

Toby: There's no point in taking him to the vet, Trudy. No-one can bring Peter back to life. He is well and truly dead.

(Puppets exit.)

THE FORGIVING KING

Trudy: Hello, girls and boys, have you seen my brother Toby?

I wonder where that boy is? I bet he's getting into all sorts of mischief, and being really naughty. Toby! Toby! Where are you? There's some people to meet you.

Toby: Where, where? (*Looks round.*)

Oh, hello boys and girls. Good to see you again.

Hey, Trudy, I've got something really great to tell you.

Trudy: What is it?

Toby: Ooh, it's so exciting, I just can't wait.

Trudy: What's so exciting?

Toby: Oh, just wait 'til I tell you. You'll never believe it.

Trudy: Toby! **Tell me what it is**.

Toby: OK. Keep your hair on. There's no need to get in a state about it.

Trudy: (*Through gritted teeth*) Toby, either tell me what it is that's so exciting, or just go away and leave me alone.

Toby: I've just heard that I've got a ticket.

Trudy: A ticket?

Toby: Yes. A ticket for tonight's football match.

Trudy: Is that all?

Toby: What do you mean, is that all? It's the final and my team's playing.

Trudy: Never! Your team's rubbish.

Toby: No, it's not. Your problem is you just don't understand football.

Trudy: Come off it, Toby. When have the Rovers ever got anywhere in the competition?

Toby: Well, they never have before. But that's what makes it so exciting. This year they're in the final. And I'm going to be there.

Trudy: Does Dad know?

Toby: What do you mean, does Dad know?

Trudy: Has Dad said you can go?

Toby: Oh, Dad won't mind. He'll let me go. Percy will be so jealous. He's been trying for a ticket for ages - and he didn't get one. Ooh, I'm so excited.

Trudy: Don't get too excited, Toby. You really should check with Dad first. After all, last time you wanted to go to a football match, Dad said no, because of all those rough people that go, and the fights and things.

Toby: This is different, Trudy. It's the final.

Trudy: How does that change things? I'd have thought the final would be even worse with peope fighting.

Toby: You're a girl, so you just don't understand.

Trudy: I understand that Dad said no last time - and he probably will again.

Toby: What does Dad know about it, anyway? Just because he's my father it doesn't mean he's got the right to tell me what to do!

Trudy:	Toby, you mustn't say that.
Toby:	Well, I'm going anyway, whatever Dad says.
Trudy:	You are silly, Toby. Dad knows best.
Toby:	Look, stop getting so upset. Nothing's going to happen.
Trudy:	But what are you going to say to Dad?
Toby:	Nothing. He'll only worry if he knows, so I just shan't tell him.
Trudy:	Toby! You can't go without asking Dad first.
Toby:	Yes, I can.
Trudy:	But you know Dad'll say no.
Toby:	No I don't. And he hasn't said no, so there.
Trudy:	That's only because you haven't asked him. Toby, please listen to Dad. He does know best.
Toby:	Listen, clothhead, I have got a ticket for the football match this evening and I am going. Is that clear? (*Exits*)
Trudy:	I do hope he's alright. One of Dad's friends got hurt the other month when he went to a football match. (*Exits*)
Leader:	Later that evening.
Trudy:	(*Pacing backwards and forwards*) I do hope Toby is alright. It's 9 o'clock and the football match finished ages ago. Dad was awfully cross when he heard that Toby had gone. He's going to get into real trouble when he gets back.
	(*Toby enters, very excited.*)
Toby:	We won! It was great.
Trudy:	Dad wants to see you. He's ever so cross.
Toby:	That's all right. I'll just go and tell him I'm really sorry and I'll never do it again.
Trudy:	Bet you'll still get punished.
Toby:	Not if I sound sad enough. (*In a sorry voice*) Oh, Dad, I'm **so** sorry. Please forgive me. I'll **never** do it again.
Trudy:	Do you mean it?
Toby:	Of course not. I'm going again next week. (*Exits, followed by Trudy.*)

Contents (in Bible Order)

Contents (in On The Way for 3-9s Order)

Subject Index

Subject Index

Notes

Notes

Notes

Children can and should be taught from the very earliest age about the God who made them and loves them. For this purpose TnT Ministries have developed a comprehensive range of teaching materials. As well as explaining the fundamental truths of the Christian message this material has been specifically designed for every age group from toddlers to teenagers. There are stories, activities and craft ideas as well as lesson plans and Bible study notes to help teachers understand the scripture passages. Teachers and children will enjoy learning more about God through his word.

TnT materials are thoroughly tested by churches and teachers around the world. They are intelligible, biblically accurate and help to make teaching children enjoyable.

Pre-school: Three books - Beginning with the Bible First Class; Beginning with the Bible Old Testament; Beginning with the Bible New Testament.

3-9's: Fourteen books covering all the major doctrines of the Christian faith.

9-11's: Six books giving children a solid introduction to Bible study.

11-14's Six books to challenge and stimulate teenagers to study the Bible for themselves.

 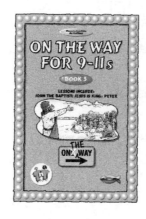 

The Game is Up
OLD TESTAMENT
Book 1 and Book 2

Take the Bible seriously and have loads of fun while you are at it!

Are you looking to add another dimension to your teaching? Do you want to encourage your children to read the Bible? Do you want them to have strong Biblical foundations without compromising on fun and activity? TnT have developed The Game Is Up for this very purpose.

All the games are directly linked to the lessons with strong Biblical emphasis that covers all major Christian doctrines. Visual aids for photocopying and clearly explained teaching points make this an excellent addition to any church resource library.

Book 1: Genesis, Exodus, Numbers and Joshua.

Book 2: Judges, Ruth, 1 & 2 Samuel, 1 & 2 Kings, 2 Chronicles, Nehemiah, Esther, Job, Jeremiah, Daniel, Jonah.

☺ The successful On the Way series continued with extra games and activities.
☺ Book 1: 80 game selections;
☺ Book 2: 96 game selections
☺ Flexible enough to be used with any curriculum
☺ Strong Biblical Emphasis
☺ Multi age (3-11s)
☺ Ideal for Holiday Bible Club; Vacation Bible School

The Game is Up
NEW TESTAMENT
Book 3 and Book 4

Take the bible seriously and have loads of fun while you are at it!

This will add another dimension to your teaching, encouraging the children to read the Bible and have firm foundations without compromising on fun and activity.

'The Game Is Up' clearly explains the teaching points, covers all major Christian doctrines and is reproducible. There are visual aids, puppet sketches and scripts.

Book 3: Matthew, Mark and John.

Book 4: Luke and Acts.

QUOTES

Biblical ignorance is a plague not only in the land but in the churches. This material will cure the problem by giving children firm foundations in scriptural knowledge from their earliest years.

Dick Lucas
St. Helen's Bishopgate

The mission zone is a flexible action pack of teaching materials, activities and tools to teach children about world missions in a fun and non-threatening, non-emotionally coercive way.

World mission is often neglected in Sunday School and other youth teaching materials. It is sometimes seen as a 'specialist' subject despite its presence from Genesis to Revelation.

This pack supplements a normal teaching program and is intended for:

6-11 year olds

Mission Sundays at church

Practical spot at summer camp

Motivating your youth group to practical action

Broadening the horizons of your school group.

If you think that 'Mission' is not high enough on the agenda of your church then this is the way to start building from the ground up.

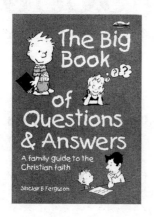

What people said about
Sinclair Ferguson's book:
The Big Book of Questions and Answers
A Family Guide to the Christian Faith

'A book providing the answers to some of the many questions which children are bound to raise when learning about Christianity. It is an ideal resource for parents to teach their child(ren) about Christianity.'

CY Magazine
Church Pastoral Aid Society

'It is Biblically sound, with well thought out answers and good suggestions for discussion, follow-up actions and prayers. The format is straightforward and easy to follow. If you have family study times this could be for you.'

Jane Rowe
CLC Book Reviews

'A book for families to discover the key doctrines of Christianity in a way that stimulates discussion and helps children want to know more.'

Covenanter Witness

Christian Focus Publications publishes books for adults and children under its three main imprints: Christian Focus, Mentor and Christian Heritage. Our books reflect that God's word is reliable and Jesus is the way to know him, and live forever with him.

Our children's publication list includes a Sunday school curriculum that covers pre-school to early teens; puzzle and activity books. We also publish personal and family devotional titles, biographies and inspirational stories that children will love.

If you are looking for quality Bible teaching for children then we have an excellent range of Bible story and age specific theological books.

From pre-school to teenage fiction, we have it covered!

Find us at our web page: www.christianfocus.com

T n T

TnT Ministries (which stands for Teaching and Training Ministries) was launched in February 1993 by Christians from a broad variety of denominational backgrounds who are concerned that teaching the Bible to children be taken seriously. The leaders were in charge of a Sunday School of 50 teachers at St Helen's Bishopgate, an evangelical church in the city of London, for 13 years, during which time a range of Biblical teaching material has been developed. TnT Ministries also runs training days for Sunday School teachers.